JUST
CHICKEN

JUST CHICKEN

100 EASY RECIPES FROM INDIA

SHARDA PARGAL

Food photographs by Ashish Chawla

OOLICHAN BOOKS

This book is dedicated to my parents, late Chief Justice of India, Mr Mehr Chand Mahajan and late Mrs Vidyavati Mahajan, who have enriched my life with all the beautiful colours of the world, and to my charming grand daughter Ayesha Forbes.

Canadian Cataloguing in Publication Data

Pargal, Sharda, 1936-

Just chicken: 100 easy recipes from India / Sharda Pargal.

ISBN 0-88982-229-8

1. Cookery (Chicken) 2. Cookery, Indic. I. Title.

II. Title: One hundred chicken recipes from India.

TX750.5.C45P373   2003   641.6'65   C2002-911437-3

Published by
Oolichan Books
P.O. Box 10, Lantzville
British Columbia, Canada
V0R 2H0

First published in Viking by Penguin Books India 2003

Designed by Dorling Kindersley (India) Pvt. Ltd.
Designer: Romi Chakraborty
DTP: Narender Kumar
Printed at International Print-O-Pac Limited, Noida

contents

Rice and Roti

Accompaniments

acknowledgements

My husband, Virendra Pargal, has been my pillar
of strength. His unconditional support, guidance,
appreciation and unstinting encouragement have made
this book possible.

My best critics and admirers have been my daughters,
Dr Anisha Pargal and Anjali Forbes, my sister Rama Tandon
and my granddaughter Ayesha.

My grateful thanks to Gudoo Kapoor, who has been a great
help in the compilation of this book, and to Monica Sethi
and Manjul Kumar.

I take this opportunity to thank Jeet, Vikram, Prabodh and
Yogi Mahajan, Mrs Mirdula Bhaskar, Monica and Triveni
Mahajan, and Richa Bhaskar, who have supported all my
endeavours over the years.

My very special thanks to Mr Khushwant Singh, Mrs Bhicoo
Manekshaw who reposed faith and confidence in my
expertise, Ms V.K. Karthika for her valuable guidance,
and Sherna Wadia for her efficient editing, patience,
co-operation and valuable suggestions.

introduction

The Indian jungle fowl is the acknowledged progenitor of domestic fowls the world over. It is native to a wide region all the way from Kashmir to Cambodia, with perhaps the centre of its origin being in the Malaysian landmass.

From literary evidence, it appears that traditionally, Indian non-vegetarian food was mainly meat based. Fowl has only been sporadically mentioned. Ibn Batuta tells us that murgh kabab and dojaj or pulao with murgh musallam—roasted chicken or quail placed on a dish of rice cooked in ghee—were some of the items that figured on the menu during the Sultanate period. Abu Fazal in *Ain-I-Akbari* mentions that musamman—a fowl stuffed with minced meat and spices—was served at Emperor Akbar's court. Domingo Paes remarked on 'poultry fowls (being) remarkably cheap' in Vijayanagar. According to K.T. Achaya in *The Historical Dictionary of Indian Food*, the people of pre-Aryan times also had no reservation in eating the karugu or kozhi (chicken), as reflected in Sangam literature. Non-vegetarian food has thus been cooked, enjoyed and relished in India since ancient times.

Today, chicken is universally recommended medically for its nutritional value. It is rich in proteins, iron and vitamin B, and low in cholesterol. It is succulent to eat and easily digestible. Its delicate flavour can be enhanced and enriched with spices, herbs, nuts, etc, making it an ideal ingredient for India's diverse cuisines.

Although Indian free-run chicken are less fatty and have a better flavour than broiler chicken, the consumption of broiler chicken is recommended due to the hygienic conditions in which they are bred. In addition, their meat is tender and the cooking time is less.

Indian cuisine has been influenced over the ages by its religions, cultures, traditions and geography, resulting in a unique diversity unparalleled in the world. In the following pages, I invite you to join me on a journey, as we explore the cooking traditions of this vast and colourful country. I hope you will enjoy cooking and experimenting with these recipes, as much as I have enjoyed innovating and compiling them for you.

table of
measurements

The cup measure used in this book is an 8-oz cup (225 ml)

1 tsp = 5 ml

1 tbsp = 3 tsp

A pinch = $1/8$ tsp (literally a pinch)

A dash = 1-2 drops

All spoon measures are level

cooking techniques

Onions, ginger and garlic

Onions, ginger and garlic can be blended individually or together in a liquidizer or food processor. They should be fried in a non-stick pan, over moderately low heat in oil, as stipulated by the recipe. If the paste sticks to the pan, add a little water and continue frying to get the required colour. This paste can be made in advance and kept in the refrigerator for 4-5 days. It can also be frozen and used as required.

Dumpukt cooking

The term denotes the baking of meat in a sealed pan to retain the flavours of the ingredients. Make a paste of flour and water. Cover pan with a lid and seal lid onto pan with the paste. Place pan on a tava or griddle and cook over minimum heat. A moderately hot oven at

150°C-180°C (300°F-350°F) is a very convenient alternative. Pressure-cooking over minimum heat is also a good alternative.

Tandoori cooking

Tandoori cooking consists of marinating fish, mutton or chicken in curd mixed with spices and herbs for long hours, and then baking in a clay oven called a tandoor. Baking in a tandoor oven implies cooking with dry heat, similar to roasting or barbecuing. Since it is not possible to have clay ovens in modern homes, an electric or gas oven may be used as an alternative and I have used them quite successfully.

Grilling is done at a high temperature, so that the flavours and juices are sealed in and the nutritive value of the food is retained.

Tandoori food is fat-free and offers a simple, easy method of cooking. Served with fresh salads, it makes a delicious meal.

Usual accompaniments to tandoori food are mint chutney mixed with curd, pickled onion or onion relish and roomali roti, tandoori roti or naan.

Chicken tikka rolled in roomali roti makes an exotic snack.

Balti cooking

The traditional Indian kadhai-cooking has been influenced
by far eastern wok-cooking, so that shredded or diced
meat is stir-fried in minimum fat. Cooking time is
minimized and the flavour and nutritive value of the food
is retained.

This form of cooking has been termed balti cooking in
Europe and has gained great popularity there, because of
the European emphasis on low fat food.

Dishes cooked in this manner can be served with chutney,
pickled onions or onion relish, and naan, roti, roomali
roti, paratha, plain boiled rice or even pasta.

basic recipes

DAHI
Curd

Makes: 5 cups

1 litre milk

1 tbsp curd or lime juice

- Boil milk and cool till lukewarm.

- Blend curd or lime juice with a little milk and mix into remaining milk.

- Pour into a bowl, cover and leave to set in a warm place for 7-8 hours, undisturbed.

Note: If the milk is too hot the curd will be sour and if it is cold it won't set properly.
To make hung curd: *Place curd in a muslin bag and hang for 3-4 hours for the water to drip out. Cream cheese may be used as a substitute.*

COCONUT MILK

1 medium, fresh coconut, white part only, grated

- Soak coconut in 2 cups hot water for about 10 minutes and blend in a liquidizer or food processor.

- Strain through a muslin cloth and squeeze cloth to extract all the liquid. This is the thick coconut milk.

- Blend strained coconut with 2 cups water again and extract the liquid. This is the thin coconut milk.

Note: Thick coconut milk is usually added towards the end of the cooking process, while the thin milk may be added earlier.

TAMARIND PULP

**1 tbsp tamarind, seeds
and strings removed**

2 tbsp hot water

- Wash tamarind, add to hot water and soak for 15-20 minutes.

- Squeeze with your hand and strain out tamarind pulp.

FRESH TOMATO PURÉE

Makes: 1 cup

3 large tomatoes

- Boil tomatoes in water for about 5 minutes.

- Drain tomatoes, remove skin, purée in a liquidizer or food processor, strain and use.

CHICKEN STOCK

Makes: 5 cups

Chicken bones can be utilized to make a very rich, tasty and nourishing stock. It can be used in place of water, for soups or gravies and for cooking rice.

1/2 kg chicken bones
1/2 tsp ginger paste
1/2 tsp garlic paste
1/2 tsp salt

- Combine all ingredients in a pressure cooker with 6 cups water and cook under pressure for 25 minutes.

- Strain stock and use as required.

spice powders

GARAM MASALA POWDER

Makes: 120 gms

50 gms coriander
seeds

3 tbsp (25 gms) cumin
seeds

1¹/₃ tsp (12 gms)
cloves

24 x 1" sticks
cinnamon

15 whole black
cardamoms

1¹/₃ tsp (12 gms) black
peppercorns

- Grind all ingredients and store in an airtight jar.

KONKANI MASALA POWDER

Makes: 425 gms

125 gms coriander
seeds

2 tbsp Bengal gram
(chana dal)

2 tbsp rice

1 tbsp cumin seeds

2 tsp aniseed (saunf)

1 tsp turmeric powder

250 gms red chilli
powder

- Dry-roast each ingredient except chilli powder and turmeric individually.

- Cool, grind and mix with chilli powder and turmeric.

- Store in an airtight jar.

KASHMIRI GARAM MASALA POWDER

Makes: 225 gms

50 gms cumin seeds

50 gms cinnamon

50 gms black cardamoms

10 gms green cardamoms

20 gms cloves

20 gms black peppercorns

10 gms caraway seeds (shah jeera)

5-6 mace flowers (javitri)

15 bay leaves (tej patta)

10 gms (3" piece) dry ginger (saunth)

1 nutmeg

- Dry-roast each ingredient individually except nutmeg.

- Cool and grind all ingredients.

- Store in an airtight jar.

salads

MURGH PHALHAR SALAD
Chicken Salad with Honey and Mint Dressing

Serves: 4

½ kg chicken

1 cup diced pineapple

2 spring onions, sliced

1 red capsicum, sliced

Dressing
2 tbsp olive oil

4 tbsp orange juice

1 tsp honey

2 mint leaves, chopped

½ tsp salt

¼ tsp mustard powder

¼ tsp black pepper powder

½ cup thick cream

Garnish
2 oranges

4-5 black or green olives

- Wash chicken and cook in 2 cups water till tender. Cool, shred chicken meat and set aside.

- Peel oranges and remove pith and seeds from segments.

- Blend ingredients for dressing in a liquidizer or food processor.

- Add remaining ingredients except garnish. Mix well and arrange on a flat dish.

- Garnish with orange slices and olives.

MURGH DILPASAND SALAD
Chicken Salad with Cream Cheese Dressing

Serves: 4

1 kg chicken

1 tsp garlic paste

1 tsp ginger paste

1 medium onion, chopped

1 tsp salt

¹/₂ cup cream

Dressing
1 cup hung curd or cream cheese

1 tsp salt

1 tsp black pepper powder

¹/₂ tsp mustard powder

2 green chillies, chopped

2 tbsp chopped coriander leaves

2 tbsp chopped spring onions

1 tbsp lime juice

Garnish
1 cup chopped lettuce

3 slices pineapple

1 green capsicum, shredded

1 cup chopped walnuts

- Wash chicken and cook with garlic, ginger, onion, salt and 2 cups water over low heat for 25-30 minutes, till tender.

- Cool and shred chicken meat.

- Blend ingredients for dressing in a liquidizer or food processor and mix in cream.

- Add to chicken and mix well.

- Spread chicken on a flat dish and arrange lettuce and pineapple slices around it.

- Garnish with capsicum and walnuts.

CHATPATA MURGH SALAD
Tangy Chicken Salad

Serves: 4

1 kg chicken

1 tsp garlic paste

1 tsp ginger paste

1 medium onion, chopped

1 tsp salt

Dressing
4 tbsp lime juice

2 tbsp chopped green chillies

2 tbsp chopped coriander leaves

2 tbsp chopped mint leaves

1 small onion, chopped

1 tsp salt

1/2 tsp red chilli powder

1/2 tsp powdered roasted caraway seeds (shah jeera)

1/2 tsp mango powder (aamchur)

1/4 tsp powdered black salt (kala namak)

Garnish
2 medium potatoes, diced and fried

- Wash chicken and cook with garlic, ginger, onion, salt and 2 cups water over low heat for about 25 minutes, till tender.

- Cool and shred chicken meat.

- Combine ingredients for dressing and mix in chicken.

- Arrange salad on a platter and garnish with fried diced potatoes.

MURGH AUR RAJMA SALAD
Chicken and Kidney Bean Salad

Serves: 4

1 cup kidney beans (rajma)

200 gms chicken sausages, sliced

2 tbsp salad oil

Dressing
2 tbsp brown vinegar

3 tbsp red wine

2 spring onions, chopped

1 tsp salt

1/2 tbsp coriander powder

1/2 tbsp powdered cloves

1/2 tbsp black pepper powder

Garnish
100 gms lettuce, shredded

1 white radish, shredded

- Wash beans and soak in 2 cups water for 7-8 hours.

- Pressure-cook beans in the soaking water for 25 minutes and drain.

- Mix all ingredients for dressing in a pan. Bring to boil and remove pan from heat immediately.

- Mix together sausages, beans, dressing and oil, and marinate for an hour.

- Place salad on a platter and garnish with lettuce and radish.

MURGH AUR MAKKAI SALAD
Chicken and Corn Salad with Vinaigrette Dressing

Serves: 4

¼ kg boneless chicken

100 gms (1 cup) boiled sweet corn kernels or baby corn

2 green capsicums, sliced

Dressing
2 tbsp salad oil or olive oil

1 tbsp white vinegar

1 tbsp lime juice

½ tsp salt

½ tsp red chilli powder

½ tsp sugar

½ tsp mustard powder

5-6 basil or tulsi leaves, chopped

6-7 mint leaves, chopped

1 bay leaf (tej patta), powdered

Garnish
1 cup bean sprouts

2 tomatoes, quartered

- Wash chicken and cook in 2 cups water till tender.

- Cool, shred chicken meat and set aside.

- Blend ingredients for dressing in a liquidizer or food processor.

- Mix chicken, corn, capsicums and dressing, and chill.

- Place salad on a platter and serve garnished with bean sprouts and tomatoes.

HARYALI MURGH TIKKA
Barbecued Chicken in Green Herbs

Serves: 4

1/2 kg boneless chicken

Marinade
1/2 cup curd, whisked

1 tsp ginger paste

1 tsp garlic paste

4 tbsp chopped coriander leaves

1 tbsp chopped green capsicum

1 tbsp chopped spinach

1 tbsp chopped mint leaves

1 tbsp chopped green chillies

1 tbsp lime juice

1 tsp salt

11/2 tsp dry fenugreek leaves (kasuri methi), crumbled

1/2 tsp red chilli powder

1/2 tsp garam masala powder

Garnish
1 onion, cut in rings

1 lime, sliced

- Wash chicken, pat dry and cut into 3" cubes.

- Blend all ingredients for marinade, except powdered spices in a liquidizer or food processor to a smooth paste, and stir in powdered spices. Mix in chicken and marinate for 3-4 hours.

- Grill chicken in an electric grill preheated to 220°C (425°F) for 3-4 minutes on each side. (If your grill is not graded in degrees, then grill at maximum temperature.)

- You can also barbecue the chicken on a charcoal fire for 4-5 minutes.

- Arrange chicken in a dish and garnish with onion rings and lime slices.

- Serve with naan or roomali roti.

MURGH MALAI TIKKA
Grilled Creamy Chicken

Serves: 4

You will need skewers to prepare this dish.

¹⁄₂ kg boneless chicken

Butter for basting

Marinade-1
¹⁄₂ cup thick curd, whisked

1 tsp garlic paste

1 tsp ginger paste

1 tsp salt

¹⁄₂ tsp black pepper powder

1 tbsp lime juice

Marinade-2
¹⁄₂ cup grated cheddar cheese

3 tbsp powdered cashew nuts

1 egg, lightly beaten

1 tsp ground coriander leaves

1 tsp ground green chillies

¹⁄₄ tsp powdered mace (javitri)

¹⁄₄ tsp powdered nutmeg

2 tbsp cornflour

¹⁄₂ cup thick cream

- Wash chicken, pat dry and cut into 1¹⁄₂" cubes.

- Combine all ingredients for first marinade to a smooth paste, mix in chicken and marinate for an hour.

- Mix all ingredients for second marinade, add to chicken and mix well. Keep in the refrigerator for 2 hours.

- Bring chicken to room temperature and pierce chicken pieces onto skewers.

- Grill in a regular clay or gas tandoor, or barbecue on a charcoal fire for 6-7 minutes, basting with butter, till golden brown.

- You may also grill in an electric grill preheated to 220°C (425°F) for 5 minutes. (If your grill is not graded in degrees, then grill at maximum temperature.)

- Remove chicken from skewers, place in a dish and serve with naan or roomali roti.

ACHARI MURGH TIKKA
Barbecued Pickled Chicken

Serves: 4

1/2 kg boneless chicken

Marinade
1/2 cup curd, whisked

1 tsp garlic paste

1 tsp ginger paste

1/2 tsp black pepper powder

1/2 tsp red chilli powder

1 tsp salt

1 tbsp lime juice

1/2 tsp powdered aniseed (saunf)

1/2 tsp powdered nigella seeds (kalaunji)

1/2 tsp powdered fenugreek seeds (methi)

1 tbsp mustard oil

Garnish
1 onion, sliced

- Wash chicken, pat dry and cut into 3" cubes.

- Combine all ingredients for marinade to a smooth paste. Add chicken, mix well and marinate for 3-4 hours.

- Grill chicken in an electric grill preheated to 220°C (425°F) for 4-5 minute. (If your grill is not graded in degrees, then grill at maximum temperature.)

- You can also thread chicken pieces onto skewers and barbecue over a charcoal fire for 4-5 minutes; or roast in an oven preheated to 220°C (425°F) for 4-5 minutes.

- Arrange chicken in a dish, garnish with onion slices and serve with naan or roomali roti.

TANDOORI MURGH
Tandoori Chicken

Serves: 2

1 kg chicken without skin

Butter or ghee for basting

Marinade
½ cup thick curd, whisked

1 tsp garlic paste

1 tsp ginger paste

1 tsp ground coriander leaves

1 tsp ground green chillies

½ tsp ground mint leaves

1 tsp salt

1 tsp garam masala powder

1½ tsp red chilli powder

¼ tsp powdered mace (javitri)

¼ tsp tenderon powder or 1 tbsp grated raw papaya

3 tsp raw papaya juice

1 tbsp lime juice or brown vinegar

½ tsp red food colouring powder (optional)

Garnish
1 tsp chaat masala

1 onion, cut in rings

1 lime, sliced

- Wash chicken, drain well and keep whole, or cut into 4 pieces, or into joints, as desired.

- Make deep cuts in chicken flesh.

- Squeeze off excess water from chicken and leave to dry for 15 minutes.

- Mix all ingredients for marinade to a smooth paste. Rub marinade into chicken and marinate for 6 hours outside the refrigerator. (If the weather is very hot, reduce marinating time at room temperature to 4 hours.)

- Grill in a regular clay or gas tandoor, or on a charcoal fire, till chicken is deep red and black streaks begin to appear. It should take about 20-25 minutes.

- The chicken can also be grilled in an electric grill preheated to 220°C (425°F) for 7-8 minutes on each side; or roasted in an oven preheated to 220°C (425°F) for 12-15 minutes. (If your grill is not graded in degrees, then grill at maximum temperature.)

- Baste chicken with butter or ghee while cooking.

- Arrange chicken on a platter, sprinkle with chaat masala and garnish with onion rings and lime slices.

- Serve with naan or roomali roti.

Note: Please be sure to use food colour from a recognized and reputed brand.

TANDOORI KALMI

Tandoori Chicken Drumsticks

Serves: 4

½ kg chicken drumsticks

Marinade
3-4 green cardamoms

3 cloves

2 x 1" sticks cinnamon

1 tsp poppy seeds (khus-khus)

2 star anise (badian)

1 tsp red chilli powder

1 tsp coriander seeds

½ tsp turmeric powder

1 tsp garlic paste

1 tsp ginger paste

1 tsp salt

½ cup thick curd, whisked

Garnish
1 onion, shredded

- Wash chicken and pat dry.

- Grind together all ingredients for marinade except curd.

- Mix ground spices with curd. Rub into chicken and marinate for 2-4 hours.

- Grill in a regular clay or gas tandoor, or barbecue over a charcoal fire for 9-10 minutes.

- You can also roast the chicken in an oven preheated to 220°C (425°F) for 9-10 minutes; or shallow fry.

- Arrange chicken drumsticks on a platter and garnish with shredded onion.

- Serve with mint chutney, onion relish and naan.

KALMI BEGUM BAHAR
Grilled Chicken Drumsticks in Green Herbs

Serves: 4

1 kg chicken drumsticks

Butter for basting

Marinade
1/2 cup thick curd, whisked

1 tsp garlic paste

1 tsp ginger paste

1 tbsp grated onion

1 tbsp ground green capsicum

1 tbsp ground coriander leaves

1 tsp ground mint leaves

1 tsp ground green chillies

1 tsp salt

1 tsp garam masala powder

1 tbsp lime juice

Garnish
1 tsp powdered caraway seeds (shah jeera)

- Wash chicken, pat dry and make deep cuts in the flesh.

- Combine all ingredients for marinade to a smooth paste. Mix in chicken and marinate for 6 hours.

- Grill in a regular clay or gas tandoor, or barbecue on a charcoal fire for 8-9 minutes on each side, till done and light brown.

- Baste with butter while grilling.

- Arrange chicken on a platter, sprinkle over powdered caraway seeds, and serve with naan or tandoori roti and sliced onions soaked in vinegar.

TANDOORI MURGH PAKODA
Tandoori Chicken Fritters

Serves: 4

This recipe is an innovated one—chicken is marinated in curd mixed with tandoori masala, but fried instead of being baked in a tandoor.

1/2 kg boneless chicken breast

Oil for deep frying

Marinade
1/2 cup curd, whisked

1 tsp garlic paste

1 tsp ginger paste

1 tbsp lime juice

1 tsp ground mint leaves

Batter
100 gms (1 1/4 cups) gram flour (besan)

1 1/2 tsp salt

1 1/2 tsp red chilli powder

1 tsp mango powder (aamchur)

1 tsp ajwain

1/2 tsp garam masala powder

1/2 tsp powdered red food colour (optional)

1/4 tsp asafoetida powder (hing)

3/4 cup water

Garnish
1 tsp chaat masala

- Wash chicken, pat dry and cut into 3" cubes.

- Combine all ingredients for marinade, add chicken, mix well and marinate for 2 hours.

- Mix all ingredients for batter in a bowl and beat well. The batter should have a thick flowing consistency.

- Add marinated chicken to batter and leave for 30 minutes.

- Heat oil for deep frying in a kadhai and fry chicken till crisp.

- Place pakodé on a platter, sprinkle with chaat masala and serve with mint chutney, onion relish and naan.

Note: Please be sure to use food colour from a recognized and reputed brand.

MURGH KI CHHARRIA

Chicken Lollipops

Serves: 5-6

½ kg chicken lollipops

Oil for deep frying

Batter
150 gms (1½ cups) flour (maida)

1 tsp garlic paste

1 tsp ginger paste

1 tsp salt

1 tsp red chilli powder

¼ tsp baking powder

½ tsp powdered pomegranate seeds (anardana)

½ tsp garam masala powder

¾ cup water

- Wash chicken and pat dry.

- Mix all ingredients for batter except water. Gradually beat in water to make a batter of thick flowing consistency.

- Marinate chicken in batter for 2-3 hours.

- Heat oil for deep frying in a kadhai and fry chicken over medium heat till crisp. Drain well.

- Cover bone with foil for easy handling, while eating.

- Arrange chicken on a platter and serve with mint chutney.

Note: Chicken lollipops are chicken wings cut into two at the joint. The meat is scraped off the bone and moved to one end. These are readily available in most meat shops.

MURGH SEEKH KABAB
Barbecued Chicken Kabab

Serves: 6

You will need skewers to prepare this dish.

1/2 kg chicken mince

1 tsp salt

1/2 tsp powdered mace (javitri)

1 tsp garam masala powder

1/4 tsp powdered nutmeg

3 tsp cornflour

2 tsp powdered poppy seeds (khus-khus)

3 tsp powdered almonds

1 tsp garlic paste

1 tsp ginger paste

1 tbsp chopped coriander leaves

1 tbsp chopped green chillies

1 egg, lightly beaten

Oil or butter for basting

Garnish
1 onion or lime, sliced

- Do not wash mince.

- Mix all ingredients except egg, and oil or butter, and grind to a smooth paste.

- Add egg, mix well and keep mixture in the refrigerator for at least an hour.

- Divide mixture into 18 portions.

- Lightly grease your hands with oil. Shape each portion of mince into a sausage and thread onto a skewer. Press into a thin seekh kabab, 4" long.

- Grill kababs over a charcoal fire for 2 minutes, rotating skewers. Brush with oil or butter and grill for a further minute till golden brown.

- You can also grill the kababs in a regular clay or gas tandoor at moderate heat; or in an electric grill preheated to 220°C (425°F) for 2-3 minutes. (If your grill is not graded in degrees, then grill at maximum temperature.)

- Remove kababs from skewers, arrange on a platter and garnish with onion or lime slices.

- Serve with naan or roomali roti and mint or coriander and coconut chutney.

AFGHANI SEEKH KABAB
Barbecued Chicken Kabab – Afghan Style

Serves: 6

You will need skewers to prepare this dish.

¹/₂ kg chicken mince

¹/₄ cup grated cottage cheese (paneer)

2 tbsp powdered almonds

1 tsp garam masala powder

1 tsp red chilli powder

1 tsp salt

1 tsp garlic paste

1 tsp ginger paste

1 tsp ground coriander leaves

1 tsp ground green chillies

1 tsp powdered dry fenugreek leaves (kasuri methi)

1 tbsp lime juice

2 tbsp grated onion

1 egg, lightly beaten

2 tbsp oil

Butter for basting

Garnish
1 onion, cut in rings

1 lime, sliced

- Mix all ingredients except egg, oil and butter. Knead well to make a smooth paste.

- Mix in egg and chill in the refrigerator for an hour.

- Divide mince into 16 portions.

- Lightly grease your hands with oil. Shape each portion of mince into a sausage and thread onto a skewer. Press into a thin seekh kabab, 4" long.

- Grill or barbecue kababs for 2-3 minutes, rotating skewers and basting with butter.

- Remove kababs from skewers, arrange on a platter and garnish with onion rings and lime slices.

- Serve with naan or roomali roti.

Variation:
Afghani Geelafi Kabab: *Coriander and coconut chutney (p. 131) or the stuffing used for murgh shammi kabab (p. 30) can be filled into these after they are cooked. Use the handle of a teaspoon to insert the stuffing.*

HARÉ BHARÉ MURGH KABAB
Stuffed Chicken Kabab

Serves: 4

Mince
200 gms chicken mince

1 cup chopped spinach

2 slices fresh bread

1 tbsp freshly ground spinach

1 tsp salt

1 tsp red chilli powder

1 tsp garam masala powder

Semolina as required

Oil for shallow frying

Filling
100 gms mashed cottage cheese (paneer)

2 tbsp mint or coriander chutney

- Combine all ingredients for filling.

- Mix all ingredients for mince, except semolina and oil, into a smooth paste.

- Divide into 12 portions.

- Flatten each portion of mince into a disc. Put a tsp of filling on each disc. Work mince around to cover filling and gently shape into a flat round kabab.

- Roll each kabab in semolina.

- Heat oil for shallow frying in a non-stick pan and fry kababs till cooked through and brown.

- Arrange kababs in a dish and serve with mint chutney, onion relish and naan.

Variation:
Murgh Kofta Curry: *Shape kababs into balls, deep fry in oil till crisp, add to a tomato gravy (see recipe Nargisi kofta curry on p. 61), and serve with roti or naan.*

SHIKAMPURI MURGH KABAB

Stuffed Chicken Kabab

Serves: 4

Mince
3/4 kg chicken mince

1 large onion, grated

2 tbsp Bengal gram (chana dal)

1 tsp garlic paste

1/2 tsp salt

1/2 tsp red chilli powder

1 tsp garam masala powder

1 egg, lightly beaten

Oil for shallow frying

Filling
200 gms hung curd or cream cheese

2 tbsp ground mint leaves

1 tsp salt

1 tsp black pepper powder

Garnish
1 onion, cut in rings

1 lime, sliced

- Place all ingredients for mince, except egg and oil, in a pressure cooker with 3/4 cup water and cook under pressure for 10 minutes.

- Allow cooker to cool before opening it.

- Cook mince uncovered over low heat to dry out any liquid.

- Grind to a smooth paste, add egg and mix well.

- Mix all ingredients for filling to a smooth paste.

- Divide mince mixture into 16 portions.

- Flatten each portion of mince and place a tsp of filling in the centre of each. Work mince around to cover filling and gently shape into a flat round kabab.

- Heat oil for shallow frying in a non-stick pan and fry kababs till light brown.

- Place on kitchen towel to drain off excess oil.

- Arrange kababs on a platter, garnish with onion rings and lime slices, and serve with naan or roomali roti.

MURGH SHAMMI KABAB
Chicken Kabab Stuffed with Dry Fruit

Serves: 6

1/2 **kg chicken mince**

1 large onion, grated or ground

1 tsp garlic paste

1 tsp salt

1/2 **tsp red chilli powder**

1/4 **tsp turmeric powder**

2 tbsp Bengal gram (chana dal)

1 tbsp chopped coriander leaves

1 tbsp chopped green chillies

1 tbsp chopped ginger

1 tsp garam masala powder

1 egg, lightly beaten

Oil for shallow frying

Stuffing
1 tbsp oil

1 small onion, chopped

2-3 green chillies, chopped

1 tbsp chopped almonds or cashew nuts

1 tbsp chopped sultanas (kishmish)

1/4 **tsp salt**

1/4 **tsp red chilli powder**

1/4 **tsp garam masala powder**

- Put mince and next 6 ingredients in a pressure cooker with 1/2 cup water, and cook for 20 minutes under pressure.

- Remove cooker from heat and allow mince to cool.

- Add next 4 ingredients to mince and grind to a smooth paste.

- Add egg and mix well.

- Heat oil for stuffing in a non-stick pan, add onion and fry lightly.

- Stir in chillies, nuts and sultanas, and fry for a few seconds.

- Sprinkle in salt and powdered spices and remove from heat.

- Divide mince into 16 portions.

- Flatten each portion of mince into a round disc. Place a tsp of filling in the centre of each, and work mince around to cover filling. Gently shape into a flat round kabab.

- Heat oil for shallow frying in a non-stick pan and fry kababs till brown on both sides. Place on paper towel to drain excess oil.

Garnish
1 onion, cut in rings
1 lime, sliced

- Arrange kababs on a platter, garnish with onion rings and lime slices, and serve with mint or coriander and coconut chutney.

MURGH KATHI KABAB
Chicken Rolls

Serves: 4

Chicken
1/2 kg boneless chicken

2 tbsp oil

1 tbsp chopped coriander leaves

1 tbsp chopped green chillies

1 medium onion, sliced

1 tbsp lime juice

Marinade
1 tsp ginger paste

1 tsp garlic paste

1 tsp red chilli powder

1 tsp garam masala powder

1 tsp salt

1 tsp ground mint leaves

1/2 cup curd, whisked

Roti
200 gms flour (maida)

50 gms whole wheat flour (atta)

1/2 cup milk

1 tbsp oil

- Wash chicken, pat dry and cut into 1" cubes.

- Combine ingredients for marinade, mix in chicken and marinate for 2 hours.

- Heat oil for chicken in a non-stick pan and add chicken. Cook till oil starts to bubble on top.

- Add remaining ingredients, stir and remove from heat.

- Mix all ingredients for roti with a little water, and knead to a soft dough. Cover and allow to rest for an hour.

- Pinch off a lime-sized piece of dough and roll into a round roti, 5" in diameter.

- Roast on a tava or griddle on both sides for 1-2 minutes, making sure the roti remains soft.

- Make remaining roti in the same way.

- Spread 3 tbsp of filling on one side of each roti and roll. Wrap in foil to keep warm.

Variation: 1/2 tsp mango powder (aamchur) may be added to the marinade for extra flavour.

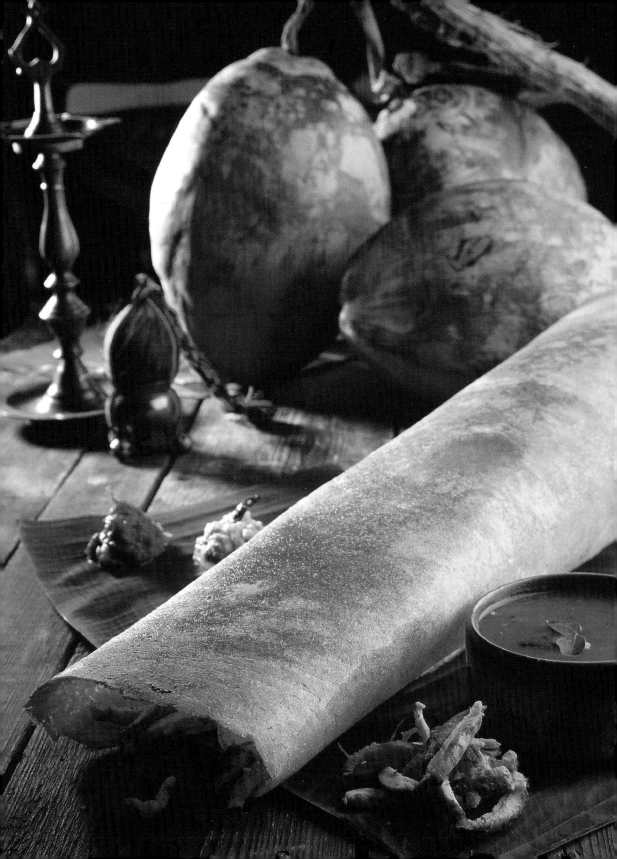

KOZHI DOSA
Stuffed Pancakes

Serves: 4

Batter
1 cup husked black beans (urad dal)

1/4 cup Bengal gram (chana dal)

11/2 cups broken basmati rice

11/2 cups boiled rice

1 tsp salt

1 tsp red chilli powder

1/4 tsp asafoetida powder (hing)

1 tsp garlic paste

Coconut oil for frying

Filling
1/2 kg boneless chicken

2 tbsp mustard oil

1/2 tsp ginger paste

1/2 tsp garlic paste

1/2 tsp mustard seeds, coarsely ground

1/2 tsp aniseed (saunf), coarsely ground

1/4 tsp asafoetida powder (hing)

1 tsp red chilli powder

1 tsp garam masala powder

1 tsp salt

1/2 tsp turmeric powder

- To prepare batter, wash both dals and broken rice, and soak with boiled rice in plenty of water for 8-10 hours.

- Drain water and grind dal and rice in a liquidizer or food processor to a slightly grainy texture.

- Add remaining ingredients except oil for frying, with enough water to achieve a thick flowing consistency.

- Whip mixture with hand till fluffy.

- Set aside for 8 hours to ferment.

- Wash chicken, pat dry and shred the flesh.

- Heat mustard oil in a non-stick pan till smoking.

- Lower heat, add ginger and garlic, and fry for a minute.

- Add mustard seeds, aniseed and asafoetida, and fry for a minute.

- Add chicken with remaining ingredients and continue to fry for a further 5-6 minutes.

- Heat 1 tsp coconut oil in a non-stick frying pan, tava or dosa pan.

- Pour in a ladle of batter and spread with a circular motion of the ladle to make a pancake as thin as possible.

- Fry till base is golden and top is soft and fluffy.

- Place 4 tbsp of filling in the centre of the dosa, fold over and serve immediately.

ANARI AKHROT MURGH
Chicken with Walnut and Pomegranate

Serves: 4

The Moghul rulers were very conscious of their health and age and the hakims tried to incorporate ingredients believed to be good for the health in their diet. This was one of the recipes created for them. It includes walnuts, considered good for the heart and pomegranate, considered good for the blood.

1 kg chicken, jointed

3-4 tbsp oil

1 tsp garlic paste

1 medium onion, grated

1/4 tsp turmeric powder

100 gms walnuts, powdered

1 tsp garam masala powder

1 tsp red chilli powder

1 tsp salt

3 tbsp pomegranate juice

Garnish
1/2 cup fresh pomegranate seeds

6-7 walnuts, chopped

- Wash chicken and pat dry.

- Heat oil in a non-stick pan, add chicken and fry till brown. Remove chicken from pan and set aside.

- Add garlic, onion and turmeric to pan. Stir and fry till brown.

- Mix in walnuts, garam masala, chilli powder and salt, and fry for 2-3 minutes, stirring continuously.

- Add chicken with 2 cups water.

- Cover pan and cook over low heat till chicken is tender.

- Stir in pomegranate juice and cook for a further 5 minutes.

- Place chicken in a dish and garnish with pomegranate seeds and walnuts.

- Serve with plain boiled rice.

KASHMIRI BALTI MURGH SKARDU
Diced Chicken – Kashmir Style

Serves: 4

¹/₂ kg boneless chicken

3 tbsp oil

1 tsp garlic paste

1 tsp ginger paste

3 medium onions, ground

1 tsp sesame seeds (til)

1 tsp poppy seeds (khus-khus)

1 tsp aniseed (saunf)

1 tsp green cardamom seeds

1 tsp red chilli powder

1 tsp Kashmiri garam masala powder

1 tsp salt

1 cup cream

¹/₂ tsp sugar

- Wash chicken, pat dry and cut into 3" cubes.

- Heat oil in a non-stick kadhai or wok.

- Add garlic, ginger and onions, and fry till light brown.

- Mix in sesame seeds, poppy seeds, aniseed and cardamom seeds, and fry for a few seconds.

- Add chicken and fry for about 10 minutes, stirring constantly.

- Add powdered spices, salt and 1 cup water. Mix well and simmer for about 10 minutes over low heat.

- Stir in cream and sugar. Cook for a further 8-10 minutes.

- Serve with roomali roti or naan.

KHUMB SHIMLA MIRCH MURGH KATRI
Chicken with Mushrooms and Capsicum

Serves: 4

½ kg boneless chicken

3 tbsp oil

1 tsp garlic paste

1 tsp ginger paste

1 tsp red chilli powder

1 tsp garam masala powder

¼ tsp turmeric powder

1 tsp salt

2 medium onions, sliced

1 cup fresh tomato purée

200 gms mushrooms, sliced

2 green capsicums, sliced

Garnish
1 tbsp chopped coriander leaves

- Wash chicken, pat dry and shred the flesh.

- Heat oil in a kadhai or wok. Add garlic and ginger, and stir-fry till golden brown.

- Add chicken, powdered spices and salt, and fry for 7-8 minutes, stirring continuously.

- Add onions and fry for about 5 minutes.

- Stir in tomato purée and fry till oil starts to bubble on top, stirring occasionally.

- Add mushrooms and fry over high heat for 5-6 minutes stirring all the while.

- Mix in capsicums and cook further for 2-3 minutes.

- Place chicken in a dish and garnish with chopped coriander leaves.

- Serve with roomali roti or naan.

BALTI MURGH KHARA MASALA
Chicken in Whole Spices

Serves: 4

¹/₂ kg boneless chicken

3 tbsp oil

2 bay leaves (tej patta)

4 green cardamoms

1" stick cinnamon

6-7 cloves

2 dried red chillies

1¹/₂ cups curd, whisked

8-10 cloves garlic

1 tbsp ginger, sliced

100 gms pickling or button onions

2-3 whole green chillies

1 tbsp chopped coriander leaves

1 tbsp chopped mint leaves

1 tsp red chilli powder

1 tsp garam masala powder

1 tsp caraway seeds (shah jeera)

1 tsp salt

A few strands saffron

Garnish
3 hard boiled eggs, cut into quarters

- Wash chicken, pat dry and cut into 3" cubes.

- Heat oil in a non-stick kadhai or wok, add bay leaves, whole spices and red chillies, and fry for a few seconds till fragrant.

- Add chicken and fry for 5-6 minutes, stirring continuously.

- Stir in remaining ingredients except saffron.

- Cover pan and cook over low heat till chicken is tender and oil starts to bubble on top.

- Add saffron and simmer for a further 5 minutes.

- Place chicken in a dish and garnish with hard boiled eggs.

- Serve with naan or roomali roti.

PAKHTOONI MURGH BALTI

Diced Chicken – Pakhtoon Style

Serves: 4

1/2 kg boneless
chicken

3 tbsp oil

1 tsp caraway seeds
(shah jeera)

2 dried red chillies

1 tsp garlic paste

1 tsp ginger paste

3 medium onions,
ground

1 tsp fenugreek seeds
(methi)

1 tsp nigella seeds
(kalaunji)

1 tsp aniseed (saunf)

1 tsp green cardamom
seeds

1/2 tsp turmeric
powder

1 tsp red chilli powder

1 tsp garam masala
powder

1 tsp salt

50 gms dry figs

50 gms stoned dates

50 gms pine nuts
(chilgoza)

1 tbsp honey

- Wash chicken, pat dry and cut into 3" cubes.

- Heat oil in a non-stick kadhai or wok and add caraway seeds and red chillies.

- Stir for a moment and add garlic, ginger and onions. Fry till brown.

- Stir in fenugreek seeds, nigella seeds, aniseed and cardamom, and fry for a few seconds.

- Add turmeric, chilli powder, garam masala and salt.

- Stir and add chicken. Fry for about 10 minutes, stirring continuously.

- Mix in dry fruits, pine nuts, honey and 1 1/2 cups water.

- Simmer over low heat for 20-25 minutes, till chicken is tender and gravy is thick.

- Serve with plain boiled rice, pulao, roomali roti or naan.

AFGHANI ZAFRANI MURG
Chicken with Lamb's Liver and Kidney – Balti Style

Serves: 4-5

½ kg boneless chicken

¼ kg lamb's liver and kidney, in equal proportions

3 tbsp oil

2 medium onions, sliced

3 whole dried red chillies

¼ tsp powdered mace (javitri)

¼ tsp powdered cinnamon

1 tsp powdered green cardamom

1 tbsp roasted gram flour (besan)

1 tbsp powdered almonds

1 tbsp powdered poppy seeds (khus-khus)

1 tbsp ground dry coconut

¼ tsp saffron

2 tbsp black sultanas (kishmish)

Marinade
1½ cups thick curd, whisked

1 tsp garlic paste

1 tsp ginger paste

1 tbsp chopped green chillies

1 tbsp chopped coriander leaves

1 tbsp chopped mint leaves

1½ tsp salt

1 tsp red chilli powder

½ tsp turmeric powder

- Wash chicken, liver and kidney, pat dry and cut into 1" pieces.

- Combine ingredients for marinade mix in chicken and marinate for 20 minutes.

- Heat oil in a kadhai or wok and fry onions till golden. Remove onions, drain and set aside.

- Add whole red chillies to pan and fry for 2-3 seconds.

- Add chicken, liver and kidney.

- Stir well, cover pan and simmer till chicken is three-quarters cooked.

- Add remaining ingredients, except fried onions.

- Continue frying over low heat for a further 7-8 minutes.

- Place chicken in a dish and garnish with fried onions.

- Serve with naan or roomali roti.

MURGH NIYOZA
Chicken with Pine Nuts

Serves: 4

½ kg boneless chicken

3 tbsp + 1 tsp oil

1-2 dried red chillies

1 tsp garlic paste

1 tsp ginger paste

1 medium onion, chopped

½ tsp red chilli powder

½ tsp garam masala powder

1 tsp salt

Garnish
½ cup pine nuts (chilgoza)

½ cup black currants

2-3 mint sprigs

- Wash chicken, pat dry and shred the flesh.

- Heat 3 tbsp oil in a non-stick kadhai or wok and lightly fry red chillies.

- Mix in garlic, ginger and onion, and fry for 6-7 minutes till light brown.

- Add chicken, powdered spices and salt, and fry for 7-8 minutes, stirring occasionally.

- Stir in 1 cup water and cook over low heat for about 8 minutes.

- Heat 1 tsp oil in a pan and fry pine nuts till golden.

- Place chicken in a dish, garnish with nuts, black currants and mint sprigs, and serve with a plain pulao, naan or roomali roti.

Variation: Roast pine nuts in a non-stick pan till light brown, to reduce the oil in the dish.

ZAFRANI BHARWA MURGH
Saffron-flavoured Stuffed Chicken

Serves: 6

Chicken
1¹/₂ kg whole chicken, without skin

3 tsp oil

1 large onion, grated

³/₄ cup curd, whisked

1 tsp red chilli powder

1 tsp garam masala powder

1 tsp salt

¹/₄ tsp saffron

Marinade
1 tsp garlic paste

1 tsp ginger paste

1 tbsp lime juice

Filling
1 tbsp oil

1 medium onion, chopped

200 gms fresh green gram (hara chana) or green peas

¹/₄ tsp salt

¹/₄ tsp pepper

Garnish
3 hard boiled eggs, sliced

1 lime, sliced

- Wash chicken, pat dry and make deep cuts in the flesh.

- Combine ingredients for marinade, rub all over chicken, including the cavity and marinate for 30 minutes.

- Heat oil for filling in a pan and fry chopped onion for about 5 minutes.

- Add green gram or peas and fry for 5-6 minutes.

- Mix in salt and pepper.

- Stuff filling into chicken cavity. Insert legs of chicken inside cavity and tie with string.

- Heat 3 tsp oil in a deep pan, add grated onion and fry till golden brown.

- Add chicken and fry, turning frequently, till golden on all sides.

- Stir in curd, chilli powder, garam masala and salt.

- Cover pan and cook over low heat, turning occasionally till chicken is tender.

- Mix in saffron and cook further for 4-5 minutes.

- Place chicken on a platter and garnish with hard boiled eggs and lime slices.

Note: Plain rice pulao can be arranged around the chicken.

MURGH MUSALLAM
Whole Masala Chicken

Serves: 6-8

Murgh Musallam was a delicacy served to the nobility at the royal court of the Sultanate Empire of Delhi.

1¹/₂ kg whole chicken, without skin

2 tsp red chilli powder

1¹/₂ tsp garam masala powder

Ghee for basting

Marinade
¹/₂ cup curd, whisked

1 tsp garlic paste

1 tsp ginger paste

2 tsp salt

1 tsp tenderon powder or 1 tbsp grated raw papaya

1 tbsp lime juice

Ground to a paste with a little water
50 gms dry coconut

50 gms (4 tbsp) sultanas (kishmish)

50 gms (¹/₃ cup) almonds

¹/₄ tsp saffron

- Wash chicken, pat dry and make deep cuts in the flesh.

- Combine ingredients for marinade, rub into chicken and marinate for 2 hours.

- Mix chilli powder and garam masala, and rub into chicken.

- Grease a baking tray with ghee. Rub ground paste all over chicken and place it on the tray. Sprinkle ghee over chicken.

- Roast at 200°C (400°F) for 15 minutes. Reduce heat to 180°C (350°F) and continue roasting for a further 20-25 minutes.

- Baste chicken with ghee from the tray occasionally, to prevent it from drying.

- Serve with plain pulao.

MURGH LAJAWAB
Stuffed Chicken Breasts or Legs

Serves: 2

4 chicken breasts or legs

1 egg, lightly beaten

Breadcrumbs as required

Oil for deep frying

Marinade
2 tsp garlic paste

2 tsp ginger paste

1/2 tsp red chilli powder

1/2 tsp salt

2 tbsp lime juice

Stuffing
150 gms hung curd or cream cheese

4 tbsp mint chutney

1/2 tsp powdered caraway seeds (shah jeera)

1/2 tsp salt

Garnish
Sliced fresh vegetables

- Wash chicken and pat dry.

- Flatten chicken breast with a blunt chopper, retaining side bone.

- De-bone chicken legs, keeping the small side bone, and flatten flesh with a rolling pin.

- Mix ingredients for marinade, rub into chicken and marinate for about 30 minutes to an hour.

- Mix all ingredients for stuffing and divide into 4 portions.

- Place a portion of stuffing in the centre of each piece of chicken and roll flesh over to cover filling.

- Chill for 15-20 minutes.

- Dip stuffed chicken pieces in beaten egg and roll in breadcrumbs.

- Heat oil for deep frying in a kadhai and fry chicken till golden brown.

- Arrange chicken in a dish and garnish with sliced fresh vegetables.

BADAMI MURGH
Chicken with Almonds

Serves: 4

½ kg boneless chicken

3 tbsp oil

1 tsp garlic paste

1 tsp ginger paste

2 medium onions, grated

1 tbsp powdered poppy seeds (khus-khus)

4 tbsp blanched, peeled and powdered almonds

8-10 green cardamoms, powdered

2 cups milk

½ tsp powdered mace (javitri)

¼ tsp powdered nutmeg

½ tsp garam masala powder

1 tsp salt

Garnish
6-7 almonds, blanched, peeled and slivered

- Wash chicken, pat dry and cut into 2" cubes.

- Heat oil in a non-stick pan, add ginger and garlic, and fry lightly.

- Add onions and fry till golden brown.

- Add chicken and fry till golden, stirring frequently.

- Mix in poppy seeds, almonds and cardamoms, and fry for a few seconds.

- Stir in milk, mace and nutmeg, and transfer to a deep pan.

- Cook over low heat stirring constantly till gravy thickens. Do not cover pan, else milk will boil and curdle.

- Add garam masala and salt, and simmer for about 5 minutes.

- Place chicken in a dish and garnish with slivered almonds.

- Serve with plain boiled rice.

Note: When cooking with milk, salt should be added towards the end of the cooking process to prevent milk from curdling.

PISTA MURGH
Chicken with Pistachio Nuts

Serves: 6

1 kg chicken breasts

4 tbsp oil

3-4 cloves

3-4 x 1" sticks cinnamon

Marinade
6 green cardamoms

1¹/₂ tsp cumin seeds

1 small, green tomato, chopped

1 tbsp chopped coriander leaves

1 tbsp chopped green chillies

1¹/₂ tsp garlic paste

1¹/₂ tsp ginger paste

1¹/₂ tsp salt

1 tsp white pepper powder

100 gms (³/₄ cup) pistachio nuts

1 cup curd, whisked

Garnish
¹/₂ cup thick cream

- Wash chicken and pat dry.

- Blend all ingredients for marinade, rub into chicken and marinate for 2 hours.

- Heat oil in a pan and fry cloves and cinnamon for 2-3 minutes.

- Add chicken with marinade. Cover pan and cook over low heat till chicken is tender and gravy is thick.

- Place chicken in a dish and garnish with swirls of cream.

- Serve with naan, roti or plain boiled rice.

KAJU MURGH
Chicken with Cashew Nuts

Serves: 5-6

3/4 kg chicken, jointed

1 tsp garam masala powder

1/4 tsp turmeric powder

A pinch of asafoetida powder (hing)

1 tsp salt

3-4 tbsp oil

1 tsp garlic paste

1 tsp ginger paste

2 large tomatoes, chopped

100 gms powdered cashew nuts

1 cup chopped coriander leaves

1 tbsp chopped green chillies

- Wash chicken and pat dry.

- Combine powdered spices and salt, and rub into chicken.

- Heat oil in a pan and fry chicken for 7-8 minutes, stirring frequently.

- Stir in garlic, ginger, tomatoes and cashew nuts, and fry till oil starts to bubble on top.

- Add coriander leaves, green chillies and 2 cups water. Cover pan and cook over low heat till chicken is tender. Stir occasionally to ensure that cashew nuts do burn.

- Serve with naan or roti.

BALTI ACHARI MURGH
Pickled Shredded Chicken

Serves: 4

½ kg boneless chicken

2 tbsp mustard oil

2 dried red chillies

1 tsp garlic paste

1 tsp ginger paste

¼ tsp asafoetida powder (hing)

1 tsp red chilli powder

1 tsp garam masala powder

½ tsp turmeric powder

1 tsp salt

1 cup chicken stock or water

Ground coarsely
1 tsp nigella seeds (kalaunji)

1 tsp fenugreek seeds (methi)

1 tsp mustard seeds

1 tsp aniseed (saunf)

- Wash chicken, pat dry and shred the flesh.

- Heat oil in a non-stick kadhai or wok to smoking point.

- Add red chillies, reduce heat and add garlic and ginger. Stir and fry for a minute.

- Add coarsely ground spices and asafoetida. Stir and fry for a further minute.

- Mix in chicken, powdered spices and salt, and fry for 5-6 minutes, stirring continuously.

- Add stock or water and simmer over low heat for 6-7 minutes.

- Serve with plain boiled rice, tandoori roti, roomali roti or naan, and a salad of spring onions and radish.

KHURBANI MURGH
Chicken with Apricot

Serves: 4

The Persian influence is very much in evidence in this recipe, where apricots from Afghanistan were used. The combination of apricots with meat is popular amongst the Parsi, Muslim and Kashmiri communities.

1/2 kg boneless chicken

3 tbsp oil

3 x 1" sticks cinnamon

3 green cardamoms

3 cloves

1 tsp garlic paste

1 tsp ginger paste

2 medium onions, chopped

1 tsp garam masala powder

1 tsp red chilli powder

1/2 tsp turmeric powder

150 gms dry apricots

1 tsp salt

- Wash chicken, pat dry and cut into 3" cubes.

- Heat oil in a non-stick pan and fry whole spices for a minute till fragrant.

- Add garlic, ginger and onions, and fry till brown.

- Add chicken and fry for 8-9 minutes, stirring frequently.

- Stir in powdered spices, apricots, salt and 2 1/2 cups water.

- Cover pan and cook over low heat for about 15 minutes till chicken is tender.

- Serve with plain boiled rice.

Variation: Soak apricots in water for 1-2 hours and stone them. Add the soaking water with the apricots to cook the chicken.

MURGH NOORJEHANI
Chicken with Curd and Nuts – Mughlai Style

Serves: 4

1 kg boneless chicken

4-5 tbsp oil

3 medium onions, sliced

1 tbsp garlic paste

1 tbsp ginger paste

3 tsp red chilli powder

1½ tsp garam masala powder

1½ tsp salt

1 cup curd, whisked

50 gms (¼ cup) powdered cashew nuts or almonds

10-12 green cardamoms, powdered

¼ tsp saffron

1 tbsp kewra essence

50 gms (¼ cup) khoya (dried condensed milk), crumbled

Garnish
10-12 black sultanas (kishmish)

2-3 mint sprigs

- Wash chicken, pat dry and cut into 2" cubes.

- Heat oil in a non-stick pan, add onions and fry till brown and crisp. Remove from pan and drain.

- Add garlic and ginger to pan and fry for a moment. Remove from pan and drain.

- Crush onions, garlic and ginger, and set aside.

- Add chicken to pan and fry till golden brown.

- Mix in powdered spices and salt, and fry for 8-9 minutes, stirring constantly.

- Transfer chicken to a deep pan with 1 cup water, cover pan and cook over low heat till chicken is three-quarters done.

- Mix in curd and cook over low heat till chicken is tender.

- Stir in nuts, cardamoms, reserved onions, ginger and garlic, and simmer for 5 minutes.

- Mix saffron with kewra essence and add.

- Dry roast khoya in a non-stick pan over low heat till pale gold. Add to chicken and cook for 5 minutes, stirring constantly.

- Place chicken in a dish, garnish with black sultanas and mint sprigs, and serve with naan or roti.

MURGH MAKHANI
Butter Chicken

Serves: 2

Murgh makhani is an all-time favourite, made popular by the chefs of the Moti Mahal Restaurant in Old Delhi, where foreigners intermingled with the local people, and learnt to eat chicken with their hands.

50 gms (3 tbsp) butter

1/2 tsp garlic paste

1/2 tsp ginger paste

1 bay leaf (tej patta)

2 tbsp powdered almonds or cashew nuts

3 cups fresh tomato purée

2 tbsp tomato ketchup

3/4 tsp red chilli powder

3/4 tsp garam masala powder

3/4 tsp salt

1/2 kg grilled tandoori chicken, jointed (see recipe on p. 19)

Garnish
3 tbsp fresh thick cream

2-3 green chillies, slit

2 tbsp chopped coriander leaves

- Melt butter in a non-stick pan, add garlic and ginger, and fry lightly.

- Add bay leaf and powdered nuts, and fry over low heat, stirring constantly till golden.

- Stir in tomato purée, ketchup, powdered spices and salt. Cover pan and cook over medium heat for 8-9 minutes.

- Add chicken and cook for 8-9 minutes further, till gravy is thick.

- Place chicken in a dish and garnish with swirls of cream, green chillies and coriander leaves.

- Serve with naan or roti.

Variation: A tsp of powdered dry fenugreek leaves (kasuri methi) can be added to the chicken along with the other spices for extra flavour.

KHOYA MURGH
Chicken in Dry Condensed Milk

Serves: 4

½ kg boneless chicken

200 gms (1 cup) khoya (dried condensed milk)

2 tbsp oil

½ tsp garlic paste

½ tsp ginger paste

3 medium onions, grated or ground

1 cup fresh tomato purée

1½ tsp red chilli powder

½ tsp garam masala powder

¼ tsp turmeric powder

1½ tsp salt

Garnish
2 tbsp chopped coriander leaves

- Wash chicken, pat dry and cut into 2" cubes.

- Lightly roast khoya in a non-stick pan till pale gold. Remove and set aside.

- Add oil to pan, heat and lightly fry garlic and ginger.

- Add onions and fry till light brown.

- Stir in tomato purée and cook till masala is well fried and oil starts to bubble on top.

- Sprinkle in powdered spices and salt, and stir for a moment.

- Mix in chicken and transfer to a deep pan with 2 cups water.

- Cover pan and cook over low heat for 15-20 minutes.

- Mix in khoya and cook for a further 5 minutes.

- Place chicken in a dish, garnish with coriander leaves and serve with plain boiled rice or naan.

SANDLI MURGH

Saffron-flavoured Chicken

Serves: 6

This recipe for sandli murgh is a special family one and has its origin in Persia and Afghanistan. It is an exotic preparation, and can be made even richer by increasing the quantity of almonds and melon seeds.

1 kg boneless chicken

3 tbsp ghee or oil

1 tsp garlic paste

1 tsp ginger paste

3 cups milk

1 tsp salt

1 tsp garam masala powder

½ tsp saffron

½ tsp powdered nutmeg

½ tsp powdered mace (javitri)

Ground to a smooth paste
20 gms (2 tbsp) poppy seeds (khus-khus)

20 gms (2 tbsp) char magaz (melon, cucumber and pumpkin seeds)

100 gms (¾ cup) blanched almonds

12 green cardamoms

- Wash chicken, pat dry and cut into 3" cubes.

- Heat ghee or oil in a non-stick pan, add garlic, ginger and chicken, and fry till brown.

- Mix in ground paste and fry for 2-3 minutes.

- Transfer to a deep pan and add milk. Cook over low heat till gravy thickens, stirring all the while to prevent milk from curdling.

- Add salt, garam masala, saffron, nutmeg and mace. Cook till ghee or oil starts to bubble on top.

- Serve with plain boiled rice or naan.

MURGH DO PIAZA
Chicken in Onion Gravy

Serves: 2

This dish originated in the royal kitchens of Emperor Akbar, according to the Ain-I-Akbari. Edward Terry, in the reign of Jehangir lauded the dish as 'the most savoury dish I have tasted.'

½ kg chicken, jointed

3-4 tbsp oil

1 tsp garlic paste

1 tsp ginger paste

½ kg (4 large) onions, ½ grated and half sliced

1 tsp red chilli powder

1 tsp garam masala powder

¼ tsp turmeric powder

1 tsp salt

1 tbsp chopped green chillies

1 tbsp chopped coriander leaves

1 cup curd

- Wash chicken and pat dry.

- Heat oil in a non-stick pan, add garlic, ginger and sliced onions, and fry till golden.

- Add chicken and fry for 8-9 minutes, stirring constantly.

- Sprinkle in powdered spices and salt, and fry for a few seconds.

- Mix in green chillies, coriander leaves and curd.

- Add 1 cup water, cover pan and cook for 20 minutes.

- Stir in grated onions and cook over low heat for 8-10 minutes further.

- Serve with naan or roti.

DAL MURGH
Chicken with Lentils

Serves: 6

The combination of dal and meat is popular in most Indian communities.

1 kg chicken, jointed

1/2 cup pigeon peas (toover or arhar)

1/2 cup husked Egyptian lentils (masoor dal)

3 tbsp oil

3 medium onions, grated

11/2 tsp garlic paste

11/2 tsp ginger paste

11/2 tsp red chilli powder

1 tsp garam masala powder

1/2 tsp turmeric powder

11/2 tsp salt

11/2 cups blanched, peeled and chopped tomatoes

2 tbsp tamarind pulp

- Wash chicken and pat dry.

- Wash dals and cook with 4 cups water over low heat till tender. Purée in a food processor.

- Heat oil in a non-stick pan, add onions, garlic and ginger, and fry till brown.

- Add chicken and fry, stirring constantly till light brown.

- Sprinkle in powdered spices and salt, and fry gently for 2-3 minutes.

- Mix in tomatoes and continue frying till oil starts to bubble on top.

- Add 2 cups water and cook till chicken is half done.

- Mix in dal purée and cook till chicken is tender.

- Add tamarind pulp, mix well and cook further for 5-6 minutes.

- Serve with plain boiled rice.

MURGH ZALFRAZIE
Chicken Curry Laced with Eggs

Serves: 4

½ kg boneless chicken

3 tbsp oil

1 tsp garlic paste

1 tsp ginger paste

2 medium onions, grated

¾ cup fresh tomato purée

1 tsp garam masala powder

1½ tsp red chilli powder

½ tsp turmeric powder

1 tsp salt

2 eggs, lightly beaten

- Wash chicken, pat dry and cut into 2" cubes.

- Heat oil in a non-stick pan, add garlic, ginger and onions, and fry till golden brown.

- Add tomato purée and fry till oil starts to bubble on top.

- Sprinkle in powdered spices and salt, and fry for a moment. Add chicken and continue frying for 6-7 minutes.

- Transfer to a deep pan. Stir in 3 cups water, cover pan and cook over low heat for 10 minutes.

- Remove pan from heat. Gradually add eggs to the hot gravy stirring constantly to attain a lacy effect.

- Serve with naan or roti.

SHIKAMPURI MURGH KOFTA
Stuffed Chicken Meatball Curry

Serves: 6

The recipe is an innovated one and the dish is delicious!

Kofta
3/4 kg chicken mince

1 tsp garlic paste

1 large onion, grated

1/2 tsp red chilli powder

1 tsp garam masala powder

2 tbsp Bengal gram (chana dal)

1/2 tsp salt

1 egg, lightly beaten

Oil for deep frying

Filling
200 gms (3/4 cup) hung curd or cream cheese

2 tbsp ground mint leaves

1 tsp salt

1 tsp black pepper powder

Gravy
1 1/2 cups grated fresh coconut

3 tbsp oil

1 tsp garlic paste

1 tsp ginger paste

1 medium onion, grated

2 tsp coriander powder

2 tsp cumin powder

Kofta

- Place all ingredients for kofta, except egg and oil, in a pan with 3/4 cup water and cook over low heat till dry.

- Grind to a smooth paste and mix in egg.

- Mix all ingredients for filling.

- Divide ground mince into 16 portions.

- Flatten each portion into a round disc. Place 2 tsp filling on each disc. Work mince around to cover filling and shape into round balls.

- Heat oil for deep frying and fry kofta till light brown.

Gravy

- Blend coconut for gravy with 3 cups hot water in a liquidizer or food processor. Strain and reserve coconut milk.

- Heat oil in a non-stick pan, add garlic, ginger and onion, and fry till brown.

- Mix in powdered spices, salt, bay leaves and coconut milk. Cook over low heat for 20 minutes, stirring constantly.

1 tsp garam masala powder

1 tsp red chilli powder

¼ tsp turmeric powder

1 tsp salt

2 bay leaves (tej patta)

Garnish
1 tbsp chopped mint leaves

- Gently add koftas.

- Place curry in a dish, taking care not to break koftas.

- Garnish with mint leaves and serve with plain boiled rice or naan.

NARGISI MURGH KOFTA CURRY
Scotch Eggs – Mughlai Style

Serves: 4

Kofta
½ kg chicken mince

2 tbsp Bengal gram (chana dal)

1 medium onion, grated

1 tsp garlic paste

1 tsp ginger paste

½ tsp salt

½ tsp red chilli powder

1 tbsp chopped coriander leaves

2 green chillies, chopped

½ tsp garam masala powder

1 egg, lightly beaten

8 hard boiled eggs

Oil for deep frying

Kofta

- Wash mince and dal.

- Place first 7 ingredients for kofta in a pressure cooker with ½ cup water. Mix well and cook under pressure for about 8 minutes.

- Allow cooker to cool before opening it.

- Place cooker over medium heat and dry out liquid.

- Add coriander leaves, green chillies and garam masala. Mix well and grind to a paste.

- Mix in beaten egg and divide mixture into 8 portions.

Gravy

2 tbsp oil

1/2 tsp garlic paste

1/2 tsp ginger paste

1 medium onion, grated

1 tsp red chilli powder

1/4 tsp garam masala powder

1 tsp salt

2 tsp powdered cashew nuts

2 tsp powdered poppy seeds (khus-khus)

1 tbsp ground dry coconut

3/4 cup fresh tomato purée

1/4 tsp saffron

Garnish

4 tbsp thick cream

2 sheets silver leaf (chandi ka varak)

- Flatten each portion into a disc. Place a hard boiled egg in the centre. Work mince around egg to cover completely.

- Heat oil for deep frying in a kadhai and fry koftas till brown. Drain and set aside.

Gravy

- Heat oil for gravy in a non-stick pan. Add garlic and ginger and fry lightly. Add onion and fry till golden brown.

- Mix in powdered spices and salt, and fry for a minute.

- Add cashew nuts, poppy seeds and coconut, and fry for a few seconds.

- Stir in tomato purée and fry till oil starts to bubble on top.

- Transfer to a deep pan. Add 1 1/2 cups water, cover pan and cook over medium heat for 12-15 minutes. The gravy should have a thick flowing consistency.

- Add saffron and stir.

- Cut koftas in half lengthwise and place gently in hot gravy, egg side up.

- Transfer to a dish, taking care not to break koftas.

- Garnish with swirls of cream and silver leaf, and serve with plain boiled rice or naan.

KASHMIRI MURGH ROGAN JOSH
Chicken in Tomato and Curd Gravy – Kashmir Style

Serves: 3-4

As in the case of most Indian dishes, rogan josh today has many variations. The original Kashmiri rogan josh, as made by the Hindu Kashmiris, consisted of meat fried in ghee with spices and curd, and coloured with dried coxcomb flowers, which also has cooling properties. The Muslims started adding garlic and onions and the Moghuls finally influenced the dish so that it became a combination of curd, tomato and Kashmiri spices.

700 gms chicken, jointed

4 tbsp oil

1 tsp garlic paste

2 medium onions, grated or ground

¼ tsp asafoetida powder (hing)

1 tsp Kashmiri garam masala powder

1 tbsp ginger powder (saunth)

1½ tsp powdered aniseed (saunf)

1 tsp powdered poppy seeds (khus-khus)

1½ tsp red chilli powder

½ tsp turmeric powder

1 tsp salt

1 cup fresh tomato purée

1 cup thick curd, whisked

1 tbsp chopped coriander leaves

- Wash chicken and pat dry.
- Heat oil in a pan, add garlic and fry lightly.
- Add onions and fry till golden brown.
- Add chicken and fry, turning constantly till pale gold.
- Sprinkle in powdered spices and salt, stir well and fry for a few seconds.
- Stir in tomato purée and continue cooking till oil starts to bubble on top.
- Mix in curd, coriander leaves, green chillies, fenugreek leaves and 1 cup water.
- Cover pan and cook over low heat till chicken is tender and gravy is thick.

1 tbsp chopped green chillies

1 tbsp dry fenugreek leaves (kasuri methi)

Garnish
2 tbsp sultanas (kishmish)

2 tbsp almonds, blanched, peeled and slivered

- Place chicken in a dish and garnish with sultanas and almonds.

- Serve with naan.

KASHMIRI KALMI - KARBARGAH MASALA
Chicken Drumsticks – Kashmir Style

Serves: 2-3

1/2 kg chicken drumsticks

1/4 litre milk

11/2 tsp ginger powder (saunth)

1 tbsp powdered aniseed (saunf)

1/2 tsp red chilli powder

2-3 cloves

2-3 x 1" sticks cinnamon

2-3 green cardamoms

1 cup thick curd, whisked

1/2 tsp salt

1/2 tsp powdered caraway seeds (shah jeera)

1/2 tsp Kashmiri garam masala powder

Oil for shallow frying

- Wash chicken and pat dry.

- Place chicken in a pan with milk, ginger powder, aniseed, chilli powder and whole spices, and cook till chicken is tender and liquid has evaporated. Cool.

- Whip curd with salt, caraway seed powder and garam masala in a bowl.

- Heat oil for shallow frying in a non-stick pan, dip chicken into curd mixture and fry till golden brown.

- Serve with a chutney.

KASHMIRI MURGH - GOSHTABA MASALA
Chicken Meatballs in Curd Gravy

Serves: 5-6

To achieve the silky texture of these koftas is the ultimate perfection of skill, and this curry is unmatched by any other kofta curry.

³/4 kg chicken mince

2 eggs, lightly beaten

1 tsp garlic paste

1 tsp ginger paste

Seeds of 4-5 green cardamoms

1 tsp salt

2 tbsp ginger powder (saunth)

3 tbsp powdered aniseed (saunf)

12 dry apricots, stoned and chopped

3 tbsp oil

¼ tsp asafoetida powder (hing)

2 bay leaves (tej patta)

1 tsp caraway seeds (shah jeera)

½ kg (2¼ cups) curd, whisked

1 tbsp Kashmiri garam masala powder

¼ tsp saffron

- Mix mince with eggs, garlic, ginger, cardamom, ¹/2 tsp salt, 1 tsp ginger powder and 1 tsp aniseed powder.

- Grind to a smooth paste.

- Divide mixture into egg-sized portions.

- Flatten each portion into a disc. Place a little apricot on each disc and work mince around apricot to shape into a ball.

- Bring 3 cups water to boil in a pan.

- Gently immerse koftas and boil for 8-9 minutes.

- Remove koftas carefully from pan, drain and set aside. Retain ¹/2 cup water.

- Heat oil in another pan, add asafoetida, bay leaves and caraway seeds, and fry for a few seconds.

- Mix in curd, garam masala and remaining salt, ginger powder and aniseed powder. Stir and cook till gravy comes to boil.

- Carefully add koftas with reserved water and saffron. Cover pan and simmer over low heat till gravy is thick.

- Serve with plain boiled rice.

YAKHANI KASHMIRI MURGH
Chicken Curry – Kashmir Style

Serves: 2

½ kg chicken, jointed

3-4 tbsp oil

1 tsp garlic paste

3 medium onions, grated or ground

3-4 cloves

3-4 x 1" sticks cinnamon

3-4 whole black peppercorns

1 tsp salt

1 tsp Kashmiri garam masala powder

1 tbsp ginger powder (saunth)

2 tsp powdered aniseed (saunf)

¼ tsp asafoetida powder (hing)

1½ cups thick curd, whisked

Garnish
2-3 green chillies, sliced

½ tsp caraway seeds (shah jeera)

- Wash chicken and pat dry.

- Heat oil in a non-stick pan, add garlic and fry lightly.

- Add onions and fry till pale gold.

- Mix in chicken and whole spices, and fry for 7-8 minutes.

- Sprinkle in salt and powdered spices, and stir for a moment.

- Add curd and mix well.

- Cover pan and cook over low heat till chicken is tender and gravy is of a thick flowing consistency.

- Place chicken in a dish, garnish with green chillies and sprinkle over caraway seeds.

- Serve with plain boiled rice.

KALI MIRCH MURGH

Chicken Curry with Black Pepper

Serves: 4

½ kg boneless chicken

1 tbsp oil

3 cloves

3 green cardamoms

1 bay leaf (tej patta)

1 cup thick curd

1 tbsp freshly ground black pepper

1 tsp salt

1 tsp garlic paste

1 tsp ginger paste

½ tsp garam masala powder

2 tbsp powdered cashew nuts

Garnish
2-3 mint sprigs

- Wash chicken, pat dry and cut into 3" cubes.

- Heat oil in a heavy-based, deep pan or non-stick pan.

- Add whole spices and bay leaf, and fry for a few seconds till fragrant.

- Stir in remaining ingredients except cashew nuts.

- Cover pan and simmer over low heat till chicken is tender.

- Add cashew nuts, and stir and cook for a further 7-8 minutes.

- Place chicken in a dish and garnish with mint sprigs.

- Serve with naan or paratha.

SABZ MURGH
Chicken in Green Herbs

Serves: 2

½ kg chicken, jointed

3 tbsp oil

1 tsp garlic paste

1 tsp ginger paste

3 medium onions, grated or ground

Marinade

1 cup thick curd, whisked

1 cup chopped coriander leaves

½ cup chopped spinach leaves

2 tbsp chopped fenugreek leaves (methi)

2 tbsp chopped mint leaves

6-7 green chillies, chopped

1 tsp garam masala powder

½ tsp red chilli powder

½ tsp turmeric powder

1 tsp salt

- Wash chicken and pat dry.

- Blend curd for marinade with greens and green chillies in a liquidizer or food processor to a smooth paste.

- Mix in spice powders and salt.

- Add chicken to marinade and marinate for 30 minutes.

- Heat oil in a non-stick pan, add garlic and ginger, and fry lightly.

- Add onions and fry till light brown.

- Transfer to a deep pan and add chicken with its marinade.

- Cover pan and cook over low heat, till chicken is tender and oil starts to bubble on top.

- Serve with naan or roti.

Variation:
Fat-free Sabz Murgh: *Omit the oil. Add ginger, garlic and onion to marinade. Cook marinated chicken over low heat till chicken is tender and gravy is thick.*

KADHAI MURGH
Fried Chicken in Tomato Gravy

Serves: 2

½ kg chicken, jointed

3 tbsp oil

1 tsp garlic paste

1 tsp ginger paste

3 medium onions, grated

1 tsp garam masala powder

1½ tsp red chilli powder

½ tsp turmeric powder

1 tsp salt

1 cup fresh tomato purée

3 medium potatoes, cut into halves, lengthwise

Garnish
2-3 green chillies, sliced

1 tbsp chopped coriander leaves

1 tbsp powdered dry fenugreek leaves (kasuri methi)

- Wash chicken and pat dry.

- Heat oil in a non-stick kadhai or wok, add garlic and ginger, and fry lightly.

- Add onions and fry till brown.

- Stir in powdered spices and salt, and fry for a moment. Add chicken and fry till golden brown.

- Pour in tomato purée and continue frying till oil starts to bubble on top.

- Add potatoes and fry for a further minute.

- Stir in 1½ cups water, cover pan and cook over low heat, stirring occasionally till chicken is tender and gravy is thick.

- Place chicken in a dish, garnish with green chillies and coriander leaves, and sprinkle with fenugreek leaves.

- Serve with naan, tandoori roti or paratha.

MURGH METHI
Chicken with Fenugreek

Serves: 4

¹/₂ kg chicken, jointed

1 tsp salt

1 cup fresh fenugreek leaves (methi), finely chopped

1 cup dry fenugreek leaves (kasuri methi)

3 tbsp oil

1 tsp garlic paste

1 tsp ginger paste

2 medium onions, grated

¹/₄ tsp asafoetida powder (hing)

1 tsp red chilli powder

1 tsp garam masala powder

¹/₂ tsp turmeric powder

1 cup fresh tomato purée

- Wash chicken and pat dry.

- Mix ¹/₄ tsp salt with fresh fenugreek leaves and let it stand for 10 minutes. Squeeze out water.

- Soak dry fenugreek leaves in 1 cup water for 15 minutes.

- Heat oil in a non-stick pan, add garlic and ginger, and fry lightly.

- Add onions and fry till golden brown.

- Add chicken and fry till light brown.

- Sprinkle in powdered spices and remaining salt, and fry for a few seconds.

- Stir in tomato purée and fry till oil starts to bubble on top.

- Mix in dry fenugreek leaves with soaking water, fresh fenugreek leaves and 1 cup water. Cover pan, and cook till chicken is tender and oil starts to bubble on top.

- Serve with naan or roti.

Variation: Add 2 tbsp whisked curd towards the end, to mellow down the bitterness of the fenugreek.

HARA CHANA MURGH
Chicken with Fresh Green Gram

Serves: 4

This recipe is a family innovation and produces a delicious chicken dish with an unusual taste.

1/2 kg boneless chicken

3 tbsp oil

3 medium onions, grated

1 tsp garlic paste

1 tsp ginger paste

1 tsp red chilli powder

1/2 tsp turmeric powder

1/2 tsp garam masala powder

1 tsp salt

200 gms fresh green gram (hara chana)

3/4 cup fresh tomato purée

Garnish
1 tbsp chopped coriander leaves

1 tbsp chopped mint leaves

- Wash chicken, pat dry and cut into 3" cubes.

- Heat oil in a non-stick pan, add onions, garlic and ginger, and fry till light brown.

- Add chicken and fry till light brown, stirring frequently.

- Mix in powdered spices, salt and gram, and fry for 5 minutes, stirring occasionally.

- Add tomato purée and cook till spices are well fried and oil starts to bubble on top.

- Stir in 1 cup water, cover pan and cook over low heat till chicken is tender and gravy is thick.

- Place chicken in a dish and garnish with coriander and mint leaves.

- Serve with naan, roti or plain boiled rice.

PAHADI KHATTI KUKARDI
Chicken in Sour Gravy – Kangra Style

Serves: 2

Pahadi or hill sour curries are a speciality of Himachal Pradesh. This thick sour spicy chicken curry served with rice makes a special Sunday treat.

¹/₂ kg chicken, jointed

2 tbsp rice

4 tbsp mustard oil

3 cloves

3 black peppercorns

3 bay leaves (tej patta)

1 tsp garlic paste

1 tsp ginger paste

3 medium onions, grated

2 tbsp mango powder (aamchur)

1¹/₂ tsp red chilli powder

1 tsp garam masala powder

1¹/₂ tsp salt

- Wash chicken and pat dry.

- Soak rice in ¹/₂ cup water for 30 minutes and grind to a paste.

- Heat oil in a non-stick pan to smoking point.

- Lower heat, add whole spices and bay leaves, and toss for a few seconds till fragrant.

- Add garlic, ginger and onions, and fry till onions are brown.

- Add chicken and fry till brown, turning it around frequently.

- Mix in mango powder and continue frying for 2-3 minutes.

- Sprinkle in chilli powder, garam masala and salt, stir well and pour in 3 cups water. Cover pan and cook over low heat till chicken is tender.

- Stir in rice paste and continue to cook over low heat for a further 10 minutes.

- Serve with plain boiled rice.

PAHADI MADRA MURGH
Chicken with Curd – Kangra Style

Serves: 4

Frying the curd before adding the chicken imparts a very tasty, grainy texture to this dish.

1/2 kg boneless chicken

3-4 tbsp oil

1 tsp garlic paste

1 tsp ginger paste

3-4 cloves

3 green cardamoms

1" stick cinnamon

1 tsp coriander seeds

2 bay leaves (tej patta)

1 kg (4 cups) thick curd, whisked

1/2 tsp turmeric powder

1 tsp red chilli powder

1 tsp salt

1 tsp garam masala powder

Garnish
1 tbsp chopped mint leaves

- Wash chicken, pat dry and cut into 2" cubes.

- Heat oil in a non-stick pan, add chicken, garlic and ginger, and fry till light brown. Remove chicken from pan, drain and set aside.

- Transfer oil to a large pan, add whole spices and bay leaves, and fry for a minute till fragrant.

- Reduce heat and add curd, turmeric and chilli powder, stirring constantly. Continue cooking till mixture resembles soft granules, and is reddish-yellow.

- Add chicken, salt, garam masala and 1 cup hot water.

- Cover pan and cook for 20 minutes till chicken is tender and oil starts to bubble on top.

- Place chicken in a dish and garnish with mint leaves.

- Serve with plain boiled rice or roti.

PAHADI CHHAACH MURGH
Chicken in Curd – Chamba Style

Serves: 4

This dish is a speciality of Mrs Raj Mahajan.

1/2 kg chicken, jointed

3 tbsp oil

1 tsp garlic paste

1 tsp ginger paste

4 cloves

4 black peppercorns

4 black cardamoms

1 tsp coriander seeds

3 dried red chillies

1 1/2 tsp red chilli powder

1 tsp garam masala powder

1 1/2 tsp salt

1 cup curd, whisked

3 tbsp gram flour (besan)

Garnish
1 tbsp chopped coriander leaves

- Wash chicken and pat dry.

- Heat oil in a non-stick pan, add garlic, ginger, whole spices and red chillies, and fry for 2-3 minutes.

- Add chicken and fry for about 10 minutes, turning frequently.

- Stir in powdered spices, salt and 1 cup water. Cover pan and cook over low heat till chicken is three-quarters done.

- Whisk together, curd, gram flour and 3 cups water. Add to chicken and cook over low heat for about 20 minutes, stirring constantly till gravy thickens slightly.

- Place chicken in a dish and garnish with coriander leaves.

- Serve with plain boiled rice.

KODI TAMATAR
Chicken with Tomatoes – Andhra Style

Serves: 4

1 kg chicken, jointed

4 tbsp oil

4 medium onions, chopped

6-7 curry leaves

1 tsp garlic paste

1 tsp ginger paste

3 tsp red chilli powder

1/2 tsp turmeric powder

2 tbsp coriander powder

1 tsp cumin powder

4 large tomatoes, chopped

1 tsp tamarind pulp

1 tsp salt

3 green chillies, chopped

- Wash chicken and pat dry.

- Heat oil in a kadhai or wok, add onions and curry leaves, and fry till onions are translucent.

- Mix in garlic, ginger and powdered spices, and fry till brown.

- Add chicken and continue to fry till brown, stirring frequently.

- Add tomatoes, tamarind pulp, salt and 1 1/2 cups water. Cover pan and simmer till chicken is tender.

- Stir in green chillies.

- Serve with rice.

MURGH MAKKAI
Chicken with Corn

Serves: 4

½ kg boneless chicken

3 tbsp oil

2 medium onions, grated

½ tsp cumin seeds

3-4 green cardamoms

3-4 cloves

3-4 x 1" sticks cinnamon

3-4 bay leaves (tej patta)

2 cups fresh corn, grated

1 cup milk

Marinade
¾ cup curd, whisked

1 tbsp garlic paste

1 tbsp chopped green chillies

1 tbsp chopped coriander leaves

1 tsp garam masala powder

1 tsp red chilli powder

1 tsp coriander powder

¼ tsp turmeric powder

1 tsp salt

Garnish
1 lime, sliced

- Wash chicken, pat dry and cut into 3" cubes.

- Combine ingredients for marinade, mix in chicken and marinate for 30 minutes.

- Heat oil in a non-stick pan, add onions and fry till golden brown.

- Add whole spices and bay leaves, and fry for 2-3 minutes.

- Add marinated chicken and mix well.

- Cover pan and simmer over low heat till chicken is three-quarters cooked.

- Mix in corn and milk.

- Cook over low heat for about 10-12 minutes, till gravy is thick, stirring continuously to prevent it from boiling.

- Place chicken in a dish, garnish with lime slices and serve with tandoori roti or paratha.

KHAD MURGH KEEMA
Baked Chicken Mince

Serves: 4

A preparation of its own kind; it reminds one of Mexican cuisine. It is a Rajasthani speciality and is traditionally baked in a sand pit.

3 tbsp oil

2 tsp garlic paste

2 tsp ginger paste

3 medium onions, grated

1/2 kg chicken mince

3 medium potatoes, peeled and diced

1 tsp garam masala powder

1 tsp red chilli powder

1/4 tsp turmeric powder

1 tsp salt

1/2 cup curd, whisked

1 tbsp chopped green chillies

1 tbsp chopped coriander leaves

8 thin roti

- Heat oil in a non-stick pan, add garlic, ginger and onions, and fry till light brown.

- Mix in mince and fry till golden brown.

- Add potatoes and fry till golden.

- Stir in powdered spices, salt and curd.

- Cover pan and cook over low heat till oil starts to bubble on top.

- Remove from heat and mix in green chillies and coriander leaves.

- Divide mince into 7 portions.

- Arrange alternate layers of roti and mince, starting and ending with roti.

- Wrap in foil and bake at 180°C (350°F) for 15-20 minutes.

- Slice and serve with mint chutney and a fresh salad or kachumber.

MURGHI NARCOLE RANNA
Chicken Curry with Coconut – Bengal Style

Serves: 2

½ kg chicken without skin, jointed

4 tbsp mustard oil

1 tsp garlic paste

1 tsp ginger paste

2 medium onions, grated

1 tsp red chilli powder

½ tsp turmeric powder

2 bay leaves (tej patta)

1 tsp salt

3 cups coconut milk, extracted from 1 large coconut

Garnish
2-3 green chillies, sliced

- Wash chicken and pat dry.

- Heat oil in a non-stick pan, add garlic, ginger and onions, and fry till light brown.

- Add chicken and fry for about 10 minutes, stirring frequently.

- Mix in powdered spices, bay leaves and salt. Stir for a few seconds and add coconut milk.

- Cover pan and cook over low heat for 20-25 minutes till chicken is tender.

- Place chicken in a dish and garnish with green chillies.

MURGHI GOTA MASHLA
Chicken with Whole Spices – Bengal Style

Serves: 2

1/2 kg chicken, jointed

3 tbsp oil

4 dried red chillies

6 x 1" sticks cinnamon

6 cloves

6 black peppercorns

6 green cardamoms

1 tsp cumin seeds

2-3 bay leaves
(tej patta)

1 cup curd, whisked

2 tbsp sliced garlic

2 tbsp sliced ginger

3 medium onions,
sliced

1 tsp salt

1/2 tsp saffron

Garnish
2-3 mint sprigs

- Wash chicken and pat dry.

- Heat oil in a non-stick pan, add red chillies, whole spices and bay leaves, and fry for a minute, stirring constantly.

- Add remaining ingredients, except saffron.

- Cover pan and cook over low heat till chicken is tender and oil starts to bubble on top.

- Add saffron, stir and cook for a further 5 minutes.

- Place chicken in a dish and garnish with mint sprigs.

BOHRI MURGH

Chicken Curry – Bohra Style

Serves: 2

½ kg chicken, jointed

4 tbsp oil

3-4 cloves

2 x 1" sticks cinnamon

5-6 black peppercorns

10 curry leaves

200 gms (2 medium) potatoes, cut in quarters

3 medium onions, chopped

1 tsp garlic paste

1 tsp ginger paste

½ tsp turmeric powder

½ tsp garam masala powder

1 tsp salt

2 tbsp tamarind soaked in ½ cup hot water

2 cups coconut milk made from 50 gms (⅔ cup) freshly grated coconut

Dry roasted and ground to a fine paste
12 almonds

10 cashew nuts

2 tsp sesame seeds (til)

1 tbsp powdered nuts

1 tbsp roasted gram (bhuné chané)

- Wash chicken and pat dry.

- Heat oil in a non-stick pan, add whole spices and 5 curry leaves, and fry for a minute.

- Add potatoes and fry for 6-7 minutes. Remove spices and potatoes from pan, drain and set aside.

- Add onions, garlic and ginger to pan and fry till golden.

- Add chicken and fry for 8-9 minutes, stirring constantly.

- Stir in powdered spices, salt, remaining curry leaves and 1 cup water.

- Transfer to a deep pan, cover and simmer for about 15 minutes.

- Add ground masala paste and stir.

- Squeeze tamarind, strain in juice and simmer for a further 5 minutes.

- Add coconut milk and fried potatoes with whole spices, and cook for about 10 minutes more, till chicken is tender and gravy is thick.

5 tbsp grated dry
coconut

3 tbsp coriander seeds

2 tsp cumin seeds

10 dried red chillies

Garnish
2-3 mint sprigs

- Place chicken in a dish and garnish with mint sprigs.

- Serve with plain boiled rice.

RAJASTHANI SUFAID MURGH
White Chicken Curry – Rajasthan Style

Serves: 2

½ kg chicken, jointed

3 tbsp oil

1 cup curd, whisked

1 tbsp ginger paste

½ tsp ground green
chillies

1 tsp salt

1 tsp white pepper
powder

1 tsp powdered green
cardamom

25 gms (about 20)
blanched, powdered
almonds

20 gms ground dry
coconut

½ cup cream

A few drops kewra or
rose essence

- Wash chicken and pat dry.

- Heat oil in a pan, add chicken and fry lightly.

- Mix in curd, ginger, green chillies, salt, pepper and cardamom.

- Cover pan and cook over low heat till chicken is tender.

- Stir in almonds and coconut.

- Cook over low heat for 5-6 minutes longer, stirring constantly.

- Remove from heat, stir in cream and essence, and serve immediately with roti.

SINDHI ELAICHI MURGH
Cardamom-flavoured Chicken – Sindhi Style

Serves: 4

1 kg chicken, jointed

4 tbsp oil

Seeds of 20 green cardamoms, powdered

1/2 tsp freshly ground black pepper

11/2 tsp salt

1 tsp red chilli powder

2 tsp coriander powder

1 tsp turmeric powder

1 tbsp chopped green chillies

2 large tomatoes, chopped

1 cup curd, whisked

Garnish
1 tbsp chopped coriander leaves

1 tsp powdered caraway seeds (shah jeera)

- Wash chicken and pat dry.

- Heat oil in a pan, add cardamoms and black pepper, and fry lightly till fragrant.

- Mix in chicken, salt, powdered spices and green chillies, and fry for about 10 minutes.

- Add tomatoes and fry for a further 8-9 minutes.

- Stir in curd and 1¹/₂ cups water. Cover pan and cook over low heat till chicken is tender.

- Place chicken in a dish and garnish with coriander leaves and sprinkle over powdered caraway seeds.

- Serve with roti.

SEYAL MURGH

Chicken Curry with Onions and Green Herbs – Sindhi Style

Serves: 4

In the Sindhi language, seyal, means cooking a dish with onions and herbs, and flavouring it with spices.

1 kg chicken, jointed

4-5 tbsp oil

5 medium onions, grated

2 tsp garlic paste

2 tsp ginger paste

2 tsp cumin powder

2 tsp red chilli powder

1 tsp garam masala powder

1/2 tsp turmeric powder

1/2 tsp powdered mace (javitri)

11/2 tsp salt

3 large tomatoes, chopped

Marinade
1 cup curd, whisked

1 cup chopped coriander leaves

1 tbsp chopped green chillies

Garnish
1 tsp powdered caraway seeds (shah jeera)

1 tsp powdered green cardamom

- Wash chicken and pat dry.

- Combine ingredients for marinade. Rub into chicken and marinate for 30 minutes.

- Heat oil in a non-stick pan, add onions and fry for about 10 minutes, till light brown.

- Mix in garlic and ginger and fry for 3-4 minutes.

- Add powdered spices and salt, stir and fry for a few seconds.

- Stir in tomatoes and fry till oil starts to bubble on top.

- Transfer to a deep pan and add chicken. Cover pan and simmer over low heat till chicken is three-quarters cooked.

- Add 1 cup hot water and cook further till chicken is tender.

- Place chicken in a dish and sprinkle over caraway seeds and cardamom powder.

- Serve with roti.

MURGHI NA FARCHA
Fried Chicken – Parsi Style

Serves: 4

1 kg chicken legs

1 tsp salt

Oil for deep frying

4-5 tbsp breadcrumbs

2 eggs, well beaten

Ground to a fine paste
3 dried red Kashmiri chillies, deseeded

8 cloves garlic

1 1/2 tsp grated ginger

1 tsp cumin seeds

1/2 tsp coriander seeds

- Cut chicken legs into 2 pieces at the joint. Wash, pat dry and make deep cuts in the flesh.

- Add salt to ground paste, rub into chicken and marinate for 3 hours.

- Put chicken with 1 cup water in a pan. Cover pan and cook over low heat till chicken is three-quarters done. Drain chicken and allow to cool.

- Heat oil for deep frying in a kadhai or wok.

- Coat chicken with breadcrumbs, dip into beaten eggs and fry till light brown.

- Serve with French fries and sautéd vegetables.

MURGHI NU DHAN SAKH
Brown Rice and Chicken with Lentils and Vegetables

Serves: 6

Dhan sakh is one of the best known of Parsi dishes. Its origin is probably the Iranian dish khoreste esfannaj, which is made with meat, lentils and spinach. It is a favourite Sunday lunch in most Parsi homes.

1 kg chicken, jointed

2 tbsp dhan sakh masala powder or 1 tbsp each powdered, roasted cumin and coriander seeds

1 tsp sambhaar masala (optional)

3 tbsp oil

1 medium onion, chopped

A marble sized piece of tamarind soaked in ½ cup hot water

Dal
1 cup pigeon peas (toover or arhar)

¼ tsp turmeric powder

3 spring onions with stems

1 medium tomato

1 small aubergine (baigan)

150 gms red pumpkin (kaddu)

1 small potato

2 tbsp chopped fenugreek leaves (methi) or 1 tsp dry fenugreek leaves (kasuri methi)

- Wash chicken and pat dry.

- Wash dal and soak in water for 8-10 hours.

- Roughly chop all vegetables.

- Pressure-cook all ingredients for dal with 5 cups water for 10 minutes. Cool and remove pressure.

- Blend with a beater, or purée in a liquidizer or food processor.

- Place puréed dal mixture, chicken, dhan sakh masala and sambhaar masala (if used), in a pan. Cover and simmer till chicken is three-quarters cooked, stirring occasionally.

- Heat oil in another pan and fry chopped onion till golden.

- Add ground masala paste and fry till oil starts to bubble on top.

- Mix in chicken and dal mixture.

2 tsp salt

Ground to a smooth paste
8 cloves garlic

2" piece ginger

6-7 black peppercorns

6-7 cloves

6-7 green cardamoms

2 x 1" sticks cinnamon

2 dried red Kashmiri chillies

3/4 cup chopped mint leaves

1/2 cup chopped coriander leaves

5-6 green chillies

1 tbsp cumin seeds

Brown rice
2 cups jirga or basmati rice

3-4 tbsp oil

2 medium onions, sliced

1 1/2 tbsp sugar

1 tsp cumin seeds

2-3 cloves

2-3 green cardamoms

2 x 1" sticks cinnamon

1 1/2 tsp salt

- Squeeze tamarind and strain in juice.

- Cover pan and simmer for about 15 minutes.

Brown rice

- Wash rice and drain.

- Heat oil in a deep pan, add onions and fry till golden. Remove onions from pan, drain and set aside.

- Add sugar to pan and cook over low heat for a few seconds till light brown.

- Stir in whole spices and fry for a minute.

- Add fried onions, salt and 3 1/2 cups water. Bring to boil and add rice.

- Lower heat, cover pan and simmer till rice is tender and dry.

- Serve the dal and rice with kachumber.

Note: Sambhaar masala used by the Parsis is quite different from the South Indian sambar masala. Dhan sakh and sambhaar masala are available in specialized shops, selling spices.

ALETI PALETI
Savoury Chicken Liver and Gizzard

Serves: 4

This dish is served at Parsi weddings to the family members who sit down to eat after all the guests have departed.

1/2 kg chicken liver

1/2 kg chicken gizzard

4-5 tbsp oil

400 gms (6 medium) onions, sliced

3 bay leaves

3/4 tsp red chilli powder

1/2 tsp turmeric powder

1/2 tsp coriander seeds, roasted and powdered

1/2 tsp cumin seeds, roasted and powdered

1 large tomato, finely sliced

11/2 tsp salt

Ground to a fine paste
10 dried red Kashmiri chillies, deseeded

6 green chillies

3/4 cup chopped coriander leaves

8 cloves garlic

3" piece ginger

11/2 tsp cumin seeds

- Wash chicken liver and gizzard, cut into halves and set aside to drain.

- Heat oil in a non-stick pan, add onions and bay leaves, and fry till onions are brown.

- Stir in ground masala, liver and gizzard.

- Fry over low heat tossing and turning ingredients for 7-8 minutes.

- Add remaining ingredients and stir well.

- Cover pan and simmer for 10-15 minutes, stirring frequently till gizzards are done.

- Serve with bread.

SALI MA MURGHI
Chicken with Straw Potatoes

Serves: 4

1 kg chicken legs

1 tsp garlic paste

1 tsp ginger paste

3 tbsp oil

4 large onions, sliced

2 x 1" sticks cinnamon

**2 bay leaves
(tej patta)**

**1½ tsp red chilli
powder**

1 tsp salt

Garnish
**250 gms straw
potatoes (sali)**

- Cut chicken legs into 2 pieces at the joint. Wash, pat dry and make deep cuts in the flesh.

- Rub garlic and ginger into chicken and marinate for 2 hours.

- Heat oil in a non-stick pan and fry onions till golden.

- Add cinnamon and bay leaves, and fry for a few seconds.

- Add chilli powder, salt and chicken, and fry for about 8 minutes, stirring constantly.

- Stir in 1 cup water, cover pan and simmer till chicken is tender.

- Place chicken in a dish and garnish with straw potatoes.

- Serve with roti.

Note: Straw potatoes are readily available with most grocers.

Variation: Add 3/4 tsp sugar with chilli powder if desired.

KALA MASALA KAJU MURGH
Chicken with Cashew Nuts and Black Pepper – Maharashtra Style

Serves: 2

¹/₂ kg chicken

¹/₄ kg (1³/₄ cups) cashew nuts

¹/₂ fresh coconut, grated

12 cloves garlic

1¹/₂" piece ginger

2¹/₂ tbsp coriander seeds

1¹/₂ tsp cumin seeds

4 dried red chillies

6 cloves

3 x 1" sticks cinnamon

2 tsp poppy seeds (khus-khus)

1 tsp caraway seeds (shah jeera)

¹/₂ tsp sesame seeds (til)

1 large onion, chopped

¹/₂ tsp coarsely ground black pepper

4 tbsp oil

1¹/₂ tsp salt

- Wash chicken, pat dry and cut into 8 pieces.

- Grind about 20 cashew nuts with a little water and set aside.

- Heat a tava, griddle or pan. Reduce heat to very low and add coconut and next 10 ingredients. Roast for about 5 minutes, stirring continuously.

- Add onion and 50 gms (¹/₃ cup) cashew nuts and continue roasting for a further 10 minutes.

- Remove from heat, cool, add pepper powder and grind with ³/₄ cup water to a smooth paste.

- Heat oil in a pan. Add ground spices and fry for about 10 minutes over low heat, stirring continuously.

- Add ground cashew nut paste, 5-6 whole cashew nuts and salt, and fry for 2-3 minutes further.

- Add chicken and fry for about 5 minutes over high heat, stirring constantly.

- Stir in 3 cups water, reduce heat, cover pan and cook for 10 minutes.

- Add remaining whole cashew nuts and continue cooking till chicken is tender and curry is thick.

- Serve with plain boiled rice.

PANDHRA RASSA
Chicken Curry – Kolhapur Style

Serves: 6

1 kg chicken, jointed

1 fresh coconut, grated

2 tbsp + 2 tbsp oil

2 dried red chillies

3-4 cloves

3 x 1" sticks cinnamon

2 tbsp cashew nuts

2 tbsp sultanas (kishmish)

1½ tsp salt

2 medium onions, grated

¾ cup curd, whisked

Marinade
1½ tsp garlic paste

1½ tsp ginger paste

Ground to a smooth paste
1 tsp caraway seeds (shah jeera)

1½ tsp red chilli powder

2 tsp coriander seeds

2 tsp poppy seeds (khus-khus)

6-7 cloves

6-7 green cardamoms

4 tbsp desiccated coconut

- Wash chicken and pat dry.

- Combine ingredients for marinade, rub into chicken and marinate for 15 minutes.

- Blend fresh coconut with 2 cups water. Strain coconut milk and set aside.

- Heat 2 tbsp oil in a non-stick pan, add chicken and fry till golden.

- Add red chillies, cloves, cinnamon, cashew nuts and sultanas, and fry for 2-3 minutes.

- Transfer to a deep pan and add 1 cup water and salt. Cover pan and cook over low heat till chicken is tender.

- Heat 2 tbsp oil in a non-stick pan and fry onions till golden.

- Add ground masala paste and fry for about 5 minutes.

- Mix in curd and simmer for 2-3 minutes.

- Add to chicken and cook further for 5-6 minutes.

- Pour in coconut milk and continue cooking, stirring continuously, till it comes to boil.

- Remove pan immediately from heat.

- Serve with plain boiled rice.

PATHARÉ PRABHU KOMBRI MASALA
Chicken Patharé Prabhu

Serves: 2

Patharé Prabhu is the name of a Maharashtrian community living in Mumbai. This is one of their famous chicken dishes.

½ kg chicken, jointed

3 tbsp oil

¼ tsp asafoetida powder (hing)

1 medium onion, grated

1 tsp salt

Marinade
½ tsp turmeric powder

½ tsp red chilli powder

1 tsp garlic paste

1 tsp ginger paste

Dry roasted and ground
1 tsp coriander seeds

½ tsp Bengal gram (chana dal)

½ tsp whole wheat

½ tsp mustard seeds

½ tsp cumin seeds

- Wash chicken and pat dry.

- Combine ingredients for marinade with ground masala, rub into chicken and marinate for an hour.

- Heat oil in a pan, add asafoetida and fry for a moment.

- Add onion and fry till light brown.

- Mix in chicken, salt and 2 cups water. Simmer over medium heat for about 25 minutes, till chicken is tender.

- Serve with plain boiled rice or roti.

Note: The ground masala used in this recipe is a traditional Patharé Prabhu masala.

GOAN KOMBI MASALA
Chicken Curry – Goa Style

Serves: 6

1 kg boneless chicken

1¹/₂ tsp salt

¹/₄ tsp turmeric powder

4 tbsp oil

4 medium onions, sliced

50 gms tamarind, soaked in 1 cup hot water

Ground to a smooth paste
60 gms dried red chillies

1 tbsp garlic paste

1 tbsp ginger paste

1 tbsp cumin seeds

8-9 green cardamoms

3 x 1" sticks cinnamon

¹/₂ cup Goa palm vinegar or malt vinegar

- Wash chicken, pat dry and cut into 3" cubes.

- Rub chicken with salt and turmeric powder, and marinate for 15 minutes.

- Heat oil in a non-stick pan and fry chicken till well browned. Remove from pan, drain and set aside.

- Add onions to pan and fry till brown.

- Add ground paste and fry for about 5 minutes.

- Mix in chicken with 3 cups water.

- Squeeze tamarind, strain juice into curry and stir well.

- Cover pan and cook over low heat till chicken is tender.

- Serve with plain boiled rice.

XACUTI

Thick Chicken Curry – Goa Style

Serves: 6

1¹/2 kg chicken, jointed

1 fresh coconut, grated

250 gms (2 large) onions, chopped

1 tbsp + 4 tbsp oil

¹/2 tsp turmeric powder

1¹/2 tsp salt

¹/4 tsp powdered nutmeg

¹/4 tsp powdered mace (javitri)

2 tbsp tamarind, soaked in ¹/2 cup hot water

Masala for grinding
20 dried red Kashmiri chillies

15 cloves garlic

3 x 1" sticks cinnamon

8-10 cloves

10 black peppercorns

2 tsp coriander seeds

¹/2 tbsp cumin seeds

1 tbsp poppy seeds (khus-khus)

- Wash chicken and pat dry.

- Heat a tava or griddle and gently roast grated coconut for 4-5 minutes.

- Remove coconut and roast half the onions for 5-6 minutes. Set aside.

- Heat 1 tbsp oil in a non-stick frying pan and lightly fry ingredients for masala.

- Cool and grind with roasted coconut and onion to a fine paste.

- Heat 4 tbsp oil in a pan and fry remaining onions till brown.

- Add chicken and fry for about 8 minutes till golden, turning frequently.

- Add ground spices and turmeric, mix well and fry for 5 minutes more.

- Mix in 2 cups water, salt, nutmeg and mace. Cover pan and cook over low heat for 15 minutes.

- Squeeze tamarind and strain juice into chicken. Cook till chicken is tender.

- Serve with plain boiled rice, bread or roti.

KORIGASHI
Chicken Curry with Coconut – Mangalore Style

Serves: 4

1 kg boneless chicken

1 cup + 1 cup grated fresh coconut

1 tbsp + 1 tbsp + 3 tbsp oil

10-12 dried red chillies

5-6 black peppercorns

3-4 cloves

1" stick cinnamon

1 cup +1 cup grated onions

1½ tsp salt

10 curry leaves

Masala for grinding
1 tbsp garlic paste

1 tbsp ginger paste

3 tbsp coriander seeds

1 tsp cumin seeds

½ tsp fenugreek seeds (methi)

1 tsp mustard seeds

1 tsp tamarind pulp

- Wash chicken, pat dry and cut into 3" cubes.

- Soak 1 cup coconut in 4 cups hot water for 10 minutes. Blend well in a liquidizer or food processor and strain coconut milk.

- Heat 1 tbsp oil in a non-stick pan and fry 1 cup coconut for 5-6 minutes till golden, and set aside.

- Heat 1 tbsp oil in another non-stick pan and lightly fry red chillies.

- Add whole spices and fry for about 2 minutes, stirring constantly.

- Combine fried coconut, whole spices, 1 cup onions and masala ingredients, and grind with ½ cup coconut milk.

- Heat 3 tbsp oil in a non-stick pan and fry 1 cup onions till golden brown.

- Stir in ground paste and fry for about 5 minutes, till oil starts to bubble on top.

- Add chicken, salt and curry leaves, and continue frying for 8-9 minutes, stirring frequently.

- Add remaining coconut milk, cover pan and cook over low heat till chicken is tender. The gravy should have a thin flowing consistency. Add extra water if necessary.

- Serve with plain boiled rice.

KOMBRI CHA SALNA
Chicken in Crab Masala – Konkan Style

Serves: 2

½ kg boneless chicken

2 tbsp oil

1 medium onion, chopped

2 tsp Konkani masala powder

1 tsp salt

1 tbsp tamarind soaked in ½ cup hot water

1 cup curd, whisked

Masala for grinding
1 medium onion

1 cup grated fresh coconut

1 tsp cumin seeds

1 tsp coriander seeds

4-5 cloves

4-5 x 1" sticks cinnamon

4-5 green cardamoms

10 whole black peppercorns

10 cloves garlic

Garnish
1 tbsp chopped coriander leaves

- Wash chicken, pat dry and cut into 2" cubes.

- Dry roast ingredients for masala and grind to a smooth paste with 1 cup water.

- Heat oil in a pan, add onion and fry till brown.

- Add ground masala and fry till light brown.

- Mix in chicken and fry for 7-8 minutes, turning chicken frequently.

- Sprinkle in Konkani masala and salt, stir and add 1 cup water.

- Squeeze tamarind and strain in juice. Cover pan and cook over low heat till chicken is tender.

- Add curd and cook for 6-7 minutes longer.

- Place chicken in a dish and garnish with coriander leaves.

- Serve with plain boiled rice or roti.

NARAL CHI KOMBRI

Chicken Curry – Konkan Style

Serves: 2

½ kg chicken, jointed

3 tbsp oil

3-4 green cardamoms

3-4 x 1" sticks cinnamon

3-4 cloves

2 medium onions, grated

1 tsp garlic paste

1 tsp ginger paste

1 tsp Kashmiri chilli powder (optional)

3 tsp Konkani masala powder

1 tsp salt

1-2 cups chopped tomatoes

1 cup chopped coriander leaves

1 cup coconut milk, extracted from ¾ cup grated coconut

- Wash chicken and pat dry.

- Heat oil in a non-stick pan, add whole spices and fry for a minute till fragrant.

- Add onions, garlic and ginger, and fry till brown.

- Sprinkle in powdered spices and salt, stir for a moment, add tomatoes and fry till oil starts to bubble on top.

- Mix in 1 cup water. Bring to boil and add chicken and coriander leaves. Cover pan and cook over low heat till tender.

- Stir in coconut milk and continue cooking over low heat for a minute longer.

- Serve with plain boiled rice.

KOZHI KUZHUMBU

Chicken Curry – Madras Style

Serves: 4

3/4 **kg chicken, jointed**

2 tbsp lime juice

1/2 tsp + 1 tsp salt

4 tbsp oil

1 tsp mustard seeds

15 curry leaves

3 medium onions, chopped

11/2 tsp red chilli powder

1/4 tsp turmeric powder

2 tbsp poppy seeds (khus-khus), powdered

2 tbsp seedless tamarind, soaked in 1 cup hot water

1 tsp fenugreek seeds (methi), powdered

1 tsp cumin seeds, powdered

Ground to a fine paste
2 medium, fresh coconuts, grated

11/2 tsp chopped garlic

11/2 tsp chopped ginger

400 gms (8 medium) tomatoes, chopped

Garnish
1 tbsp chopped coriander leaves

- Wash chicken and pat dry.

- Combine lime juice and 1/2 tsp salt, rub into chicken and marinate for 10 minutes.

- Heat oil in a non-stick pan and add mustard seeds. Allow to splutter, add curry leaves and onions, and fry till onions are brown.

- Stir in chilli powder and turmeric.

- Mix poppy seeds with ground coconut paste and add to pan. Fry for 8-9 minutes.

- Add chicken and fry for about 8 minutes, stirring frequently.

- Squeeze tamarind and strain juice into pan. Stir in fenugreek, cumin, 1 tsp salt and 2 cups water.

- Cover pan and cook over low heat till chicken is tender.

- Place chicken in a dish and garnish with coriander leaves.

- Serve with plain boiled rice.

KOZHI VARATHA KOSAMBU
Chicken Chettinad

Serves: 6

1 kg chicken, jointed

3 tbsp oil

2 tsp garlic paste

2 tsp ginger paste

1 medium onion, grated

1½ tsp salt

2 tsp garam masala powder

2 tsp red chilli powder

½ tsp turmeric powder

3 tsp powdered aniseed (saunf)

1½ tbsp powdered poppy seeds (khus-khus)

½ fresh coconut, ground

1 star anise (badian)

6-7 powdered green cardamoms

5-6 curry leaves

1 cup fresh tomato purée

Garnish
1 tbsp chopped coriander leaves

- Wash chicken and pat dry.

- Heat oil in a non-stick pan, add garlic, ginger and onion, and fry till light brown.

- Add salt, powdered spices and coconut, and fry for about 5 minutes.

- Add chicken, star anise, cardamom and curry leaves, and fry for 8-9 minutes, stirring frequently.

- Stir in tomato purée and continue cooking over medium heat till oil starts to bubble on top.

- Pour in 2 cups water. Cover pan and cook over low heat till chicken is tender.

- Place chicken in a dish and garnish with coriander leaves.

KOZHI CHETTINAD

Chicken Fry – Chettinad Style

Serves: 4

1 kg chicken

3 tbsp oil

2 cloves

5-6 black peppercorns

1" stick cinnamon

1 tsp aniseed (saunf)

1 tsp cumin seeds

6-8 curry leaves

Marinade
2 medium onions, chopped

1 tsp garlic paste

1 tsp ginger paste

20 dried red chillies

1 tbsp lime juice

1 tsp salt

1/4 tsp turmeric powder

- Wash chicken, pat dry and cut into 8 pieces.

- Grind ingredients for marinade to a fine paste.

- Make deep cuts in chicken flesh, rub marinade into chicken and marinate for 3 hours.

- Heat oil in a non-stick pan, add all spices except curry leaves, and sauté for a minute.

- Add curry leaves and chicken, and fry for 2-3 minutes.

- Reduce heat, cover pan and cook, turning chicken frequently till tender.

- Sprinkle about 1/3 cup water over chicken, if necessary.

KOZHI CURRY

Chicken Curry – Malabar Style

Serves: 4

1 kg chicken, jointed

4 tbsp oil

2 medium onions, sliced

10 black peppercorns

2 tsp garlic paste

2 tsp ginger paste

1/2 tsp turmeric powder

3 large tomatoes, chopped

2 tsp powdered poppy seeds (khus-khus)

2 tsp ground sultanas (kishmish)

1½ tbsp red chilli powder

1½ tsp coriander powder

1½ tsp salt

4 tbsp curd, whisked

1 tsp lime juice

A pinch of sugar

- Wash chicken and pat dry.

- Heat oil in a pan, add onions and fry till brown.

- Add peppercorns, garlic, ginger and turmeric, and fry for a minute.

- Mix in tomatoes, and continue frying till oil starts to bubble on top.

- Sprinkle in poppy seeds, sultanas, chilli powder, coriander powder and salt, and fry for a minute.

- Add chicken, and fry for 7-8 minutes stirring constantly.

- Pour in 3 cups water. Cover pan and cook till chicken is tender.

- Stir in curd, lime juice and sugar, and cook further for 5 minutes.

KOZHI VARATTIYATHU
Chicken Masala – Malabar Style

Serves: 2

½ kg chicken
2 tbsp coconut oil
1 tsp mustard seeds
2 dried red chillies
20 curry leaves
1 tsp salt
1 tsp red chilli powder

Masala for grinding
1 star anise (badian)
2 x 1" sticks cinnamon
3-4 cloves
3-4 green cardamoms
1 tbsp poppy seeds
(khus-khus)
3 tbsp coriander seeds
½ cup grated fresh
coconut

Garnish
Freshly ground black
pepper

- Wash chicken, pat dry and cut into 3" pieces.

- Dry roast ingredients for masala, and grind to a fine paste.

- Heat oil in a pan, add mustard seeds, red chillies and 10 curry leaves, and fry for a few moments.

- Add chicken and fry for a minute.

- Mix in ground paste and continue frying for 1-2 minutes more.

- Add 1½ cups water, salt, chilli powder and remaining 10 curry leaves.

- Cover pan and cook over low heat till chicken is tender.

- Place chicken in a dish and sprinkle over a little freshly ground black pepper.

KOZHI ISTU

Chicken and Vegetable Stew – Kerala Style

Serves: 4

½ kg boneless chicken

2 cups grated fresh coconut

3 tbsp oil

1" stick cinnamon

3-4 black peppercorns

3-4 green cardamoms

3-4 cloves

3 medium onions, grated

1 tsp ginger paste

1 tbsp chopped green chillies

2 bay leaves

A pinch of turmeric powder (optional)

½ tsp powdered aniseed (saunf)

1 tsp salt

5 medium potatoes, quartered

1 carrot, sliced

½ cup shelled green peas

8-10 curry leaves

4-5 cloves garlic, sliced

1 tbsp sliced ginger

• Wash chicken, pat dry and cut into 3" cubes.

• Blend coconut with 3 cups hot water in a liquidizer or food processor. Strain coconut milk and set aside.

• Heat oil in a non-stick pan, add whole spices and fry for a few moments till fragrant.

• Add onions, ginger paste and green chillies, and fry for 10 minutes.

• Mix in chicken, bay leaves, turmeric (if used), aniseed and salt, and fry for 8-9 minutes.

• Transfer chicken to a deep pan and stir in 3 cups water. Cover pan and cook for 10 minutes.

• Add vegetables, curry leaves, sliced garlic and ginger, and cook till vegetables are tender.

• Serve with rice.

KOZHI ERACHI PAAL KARI

Chicken in Coconut Curry – Kerala Style

Serves: 2

1/2 kg chicken, jointed

2 cups grated fresh coconut

3 tbsp oil

1 tsp mustard seeds

1 medium onion, sliced

1 tsp garlic, chopped

1 tsp ginger, chopped

8-10 curry leaves

2 tbsp coriander powder

1 1/2 tsp red chilli powder

1/2 tsp turmeric powder

1 tsp salt

1 tbsp brown vinegar

Garnish
2 dried red chillies (optional)

1 lime, sliced (optional)

- Wash chicken and pat dry.

- Blend coconut with 1/2 cup warm water in a liquidizer or food processor. Strain thick coconut milk and set aside.

- Blend strained coconut again with 2 cups warm water. Strain thin coconut milk and set aside.

- Heat oil in a pan, add mustard seeds, allow to splutter and add onion. Fry for 2-3 minutes till onion is golden.

- Add garlic, ginger and curry leaves, and fry for a further 2 minutes.

- Mix in powdered spices and fry for a minute.

- Add chicken, salt and vinegar, and fry for about 5 minutes.

- Add thin coconut milk, cover pan and cook over low heat till chicken is tender.

- Stir in thick coconut milk, bring to boil and remove from heat immediately.

- Garnish with red chillies and lime slices (if used), and serve with plain boiled rice.

The word pulao appears both in Sanskrit and Tamil literature. It is also ascribed to the Persian and Arabic pilav. Pulao is a combination of rice and spiced cooked meat, while biryani is a combination of spicy, saffron-flavoured meat, layered with rice. Favourite accompaniments with biryani and pulao are kachumber, pickled onions, plain curd and raita—spiced curd.

MURGH PULAO
Chicken Pulao

Serves: 4

Chicken
3/4 kg boneless chicken

1 tsp garlic paste

1 tsp ginger paste

1 tsp powdered green cardamom

2 x 1" sticks cinnamon

2 bay leaves (tej patta)

1 tsp salt

Rice
2 cups basmati rice

3-4 tbsp oil

1/2 tsp garam masala powder

1 tsp salt

Garnish
1 medium onion, sliced

- Wash chicken, pat dry and cut into 3" cubes.

- Place all ingredients for chicken in a pan with 5 cups water. Cover pan and cook over low heat for 10 minutes.

- Wash rice and soak in plenty of water for 30 minutes. Drain.

- Heat oil for rice in a deep pan. Add onion for garnish and fry till golden brown. Remove onion from pan, drain and set aside.

- Add rice to pan and fry for 6-7 minutes, stirring continuously.

- Add chicken with 4 1/2 cups stock, garam masala and salt. Stir gently, cover pan and cook over low heat till rice is tender and dry.

- Place pulao on a platter and garnish with reserved fried onions.

GOLYACHA MURGH PULAO
Chicken Meatball Pulao

Serves: 6

Meatballs
3/4 kg chicken

1/2 cup Bengal gram (chana dal)

1 tsp garlic paste

1 tsp ginger paste

1 tsp coriander powder

1 tsp cumin powder

1 tsp red chilli powder

1 tsp salt

1/4 tsp turmeric powder

1 tbsp whole wheat flour (atta)

Masala for meatballs
1 cup grated fresh coconut

1 tsp garlic paste

1 tsp ginger paste

1 tsp red chilli powder

1 tbsp powdered caraway seeds (shah jeera)

4-5 cloves, powdered

1" stick cinnamon, powdered

2 tbsp oil

Rice
1/2 kg (2 1/2 cups) basmati or jirga rice

- Wash chicken and pat dry. Debone and mince the flesh.

- Wash Bengal gram and soak in water for an hour.

- Mix chicken mince with remaining ingredients for meatballs and grind mixture to a smooth paste.

- Shape into small balls and steam for 12-15 minutes.

- Cook chicken bones with 6 cups water in a pressure cooker for 20 minutes. Strain stock and reserve.

- Mix all ingredients for masala, except oil.

- Heat oil for masala in a non-stick pan. Add masala and fry till oil starts to bubble on top.

- Add meatballs and fry for about 5 minutes, stirring gently.

- Wash rice and soak in water for 30 minutes.

- Heat 4 tbsp oil for rice in another pan and fry onions till brown and crisp. Remove onions from pan, drain and reserve.

4 tbsp oil

2 medium onions, sliced

1/3 cup cashew nuts

1/3 cup sultanas (kishmish)

3 cloves

4 black cardamoms

2 bay leaves (tej patta)

1 tsp salt

1/4 tsp saffron soaked in 1 tsp rose-water

- Add cashew nuts and sultanas and fry till cashew nuts are golden. Remove from pan, drain and reserve.

- Add whole spices and bay leaves to pan and fry for a few moments till fragrant.

- Drain rice, add to pan and continue frying for 8-9 minutes, stirring constantly.

- Stir in salt and $4^1/2$ cups stock.

- Cover pan and cook over low heat till rice is tender.

- Place one-third of the rice in a deep pan. Place half the meatballs over the rice. Sprinkle over one-third onions. Cover with another one-third rice. Place remaining meatballs over rice, sprinkle over one-third onions and cover with remaining rice. Scatter cashew nuts, sultanas, saffron and remaining onions on top.

- Cover pan and cook over very low heat for 5-7 minutes.

- Serve with a chutney and papad.

GOAN KOMBI PULAO

Chicken Pulao – Goa Style

Serves: 4

400 gms boneless chicken

250 gms (1¼ cups) rice

1½ tsp salt

3 tbsp oil

3-4 x 1" sticks cinnamon

3-4 green cardamoms

3-4 cloves

2 medium onions, grated

1 tsp garlic paste

1 tsp ginger paste

3 large tomatoes, chopped

Garnish
100 gms cooked ham, cubed

- Wash chicken, pat dry and cut into 3" cubes.

- Wash rice and soak in water for 30 minutes.

- Place chicken, salt and 4 cups water in a pan and cook over low heat for 15 minutes.

- Heat oil in a pan, add whole spices, onions, garlic and ginger, and fry till onions are brown.

- Drain rice, add to pan and continue frying for 8-9 minutes.

- Stir in tomatoes and cook for 7-8 minutes.

- Add chicken with 3 cups stock. Cover pan and cook over low heat till rice is tender and dry.

- Place pulao in a platter and garnish with ham cubes.

KOMRI PULAO

Chicken and Coconut Pulao – Konkan Style

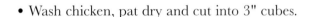

Serves: 3-4

¹/₂ kg boneless chicken

¹/₂ fresh coconut, grated

2 tbsp oil

1 tsp garlic paste

1 tsp ginger paste

2 medium onions, grated

1 tsp red chilli powder

1 tsp Konkani masala powder

1 tsp salt

1 cup fresh tomato purée

1 cup kolum or basmati rice

- Wash chicken, pat dry and cut into 3" cubes.

- Blend coconut in a liquidizer or food processor with 1 cup warm water. Strain thick coconut milk and use for any other purpose.

- Blend strained coconut again with 1 cup warm water. Strain thin coconut milk and reserve.

- Heat oil in a non-stick pan, add garlic, ginger and onions, and fry till brown.

- Add chicken, powdered spices and salt, and fry for about 8 minutes, stirring constantly.

- Add tomato purée and continue frying till oil starts to bubble on top.

- Transfer chicken to a deep pan with 3 cups water. Cover pan and simmer till chicken is tender. There should be 1 cup gravy left in the pan.

- Wash rice and soak in water for 15 minutes. Drain and add to chicken with 1 cup reserved thin coconut milk.

- Stir gently, cover pan and cook over low heat till rice is tender.

KOZHI BIRYANI

Chicken Biryani – Malabar Style

Serves: 5-6

3/4 kg chicken, jointed

2 cups grated fresh coconut

2 tbsp + 1/2 cup ghee

4-5 medium onions, sliced

3/4 kg (33/4 cups) basmati rice

1 tbsp oil

1 tsp salt

1/3 cup warm milk

1/4 tsp yellow food colour (optional)

Marinade

2 tsp garlic paste

2 tsp ginger paste

3 cups curd, whisked

3 tbsp ground dry coconut

3 tbsp powdered cashew nuts

3 tbsp chopped green chillies

1 cup chopped coriander leaves

1/2 cup chopped mint leaves

14 cloves

12 green cardamoms

3 x 1" sticks cinnamon

1 tsp salt

1 tbsp lime juice

- Wash chicken and pat dry.

- Combine ingredients for marinade.

- Blend grated coconut with 1 1/2 cups warm water in a liquidiser or food processor. Strain coconut milk and add to marinade.

- Heat 2 tbsp ghee in a pan, and fry onions till brown and crisp. Drain onions, crush and stir into marinade.

- Mix chicken into marinade and marinate for 2 hours.

- Pour any ghee remaining in the pan after frying onions, over chicken.

- Wash rice and cook in plenty of water with oil and salt, till half-cooked.

- Place chicken in a large pan and arrange rice over it.

- Mix milk with food colour (if used), and sprinkle over rice with 1/2 cup ghee.

- Cover pan and bake at 180°C (350°F) for 35-40 minutes.

Note: Please be sure to use food colour from a recognized and reputed brand.

KACCHÉ MURGH KI BIRYANI
Chicken Biryani

Serves: 4

3/4 kg chicken, jointed

400 gms (2 cups) basmati rice

4 tbsp ghee

3 large onions, finely sliced

1 tsp caraway seeds (shah jeera)

1½ cups thick curd, whisked

1 cup fresh tomato purée

1½ tsp red chilli powder

1½ tsp garam masala powder

½ tsp turmeric powder

1½ tsp salt

3 green cardamoms

3 x 1" sticks cinnamon

3 cloves

½ tsp saffron

½ cup milk

1 tbsp ghee for sprinkling on rice

Marinade
1 tbsp garlic paste

1 tbsp ginger paste

1 tbsp ground coriander leaves

1 tbsp ground green chillies

1 tbsp lime juice

- Wash chicken and pat dry.

- Combine ingredients for marinade, rub into chicken and marinate for an hour.

- Wash rice and soak in water for an hour.

- Heat ghee in a non-stick pan and fry onions till brown. Remove onions from pan and drain. Grind half the onions.

- Remove pan from heat and add caraway seeds. Stir and pour contents of pan over chicken.

- Mix curd, tomato purée, powdered spices, salt and ground fried onions. Add chicken and mix well.

- Boil rice in plenty of water with whole spices till half done.

- Drain rice, reserving 1 cup water.

- Mix saffron with hot milk and reserved rice water.

- Spread chicken mixture in a deep pan. Sprinkle over reserved fried onions and cover with rice. Sprinkle saffron mixture and ghee over rice.

- Cook on dum or bake in an oven preheated to 180°C (350°F) for 40 minutes.

BOHRI MURGH BIRYANI

Chicken Biryani – Bohra Style

Serves: 6

1 kg chicken, jointed

1 kg onions (8 large), sliced, fried crisp and drained

1/2 kg (3 large) potatoes, peeled and cut lengthwise into half

3/4 kg (3 3/4 cups) rice

1 tbsp lime juice

4 tbsp oil

3 x 1" sticks cinnamon

3 black cardamoms

6-7 black peppercorns

3 cloves

3 tsp caraway seeds (shah jeera)

1/4 tsp saffron soaked in 1/2 cup warm milk

Marinade
1/2 kg tomatoes (3 large), blanched, peeled and chopped

1/2 kg (2 cups) curd, whisked

2 tsp garlic paste

2 tsp ginger paste

3 tsp cumin seeds

2 tsp garam masala powder

2-3 tsp red chilli powder

1/2 tsp turmeric powder

2 tsp salt

- Wash chicken and pat dry.

- Combine ingredients for marinade. Crush fried onions and add to marinade with potatoes and chicken. Mix well and marinate for 4 hours.

- Wash rice and soak in plenty of water with lime juice for 30 minutes.

- Cook rice in soaking water till three-quarters done. Drain water.

- Heat oil in a deep pan. Add whole spices and fry lightly till fragrant.

- Arrange a thin layer of rice in pan and place chicken, with marinade on top. Cover with remaining rice.

- Sprinkle saffron-flavoured milk over rice.

- Cover pan and cook over very low heat for 30 minutes; or bake in an oven preheated to 150°C (300°F) for 30 minutes; or cook on dum.

- Serve with plain whisked curd.

MURGH TIKKA PULAO
Barbecued Chicken Pulao

Serves: 4

You will need skewers to prepare this dish.

¹⁄₂ kg boneless chicken

1 tbsp cream

A pinch of powdered saffron

Marinade
1 medium onion, sliced

1 tsp garlic paste

2 tbsp lime juice

1 tsp salt

¹⁄₂ tsp freshly ground black pepper

1 tbsp oil

Rice
2 cups basmati rice

1 tsp salt

2-3 tbsp butter

2 egg yolks, lightly beaten

¹⁄₄ tsp black pepper

Garnish
¹⁄₄ tsp whole black peppercorns

6-7 cherry tomatoes

- Wash chicken, pat dry and cut into 2¹⁄₂" cubes.

- Combine ingredients for marinade, mix in chicken and marinate for 2-4 hours.

- Mix saffron with cream.

- String chicken pieces onto a skewer. Brush with saffron and cream mixture.

- Wash rice and soak in water for an hour.

- Cook rice in plenty of boiling water with salt, till tender. Drain.

- Mix butter and egg yolk into rice gently with a fork. Place rice over low heat and cook for 4-5 minutes.

- Grill chicken over a charcoal fire, or in a regular clay or gas tandoor, or electric grill preheated to 220°C (425°F) for 8-9 minutes, basting with saffron and cream mixture. (If your grill is not graded in degrees, then grill at maximum temperature.)

- Place rice on a platter. Arrange chicken with skewers on top of rice, scatter peppercorns and cherry tomatoes around, and serve.

BIRYANI SHAHJEHANI
Chicken Biryani – Mughlai Style

Serves: 4

Chicken
½ kg boneless chicken

4 tbsp oil

1 tsp garlic paste

1 tsp ginger paste

3 large onions, grated or ground

1 tbsp powdered poppy seeds (khus-khus)

1 tbsp powdered cheronji (charoli)

1 tbsp powdered cashew nuts

1 tbsp ground dry coconut

1 cup fresh tomato purée

1 tbsp lime juice

Marinade
½ kg (2 cups) thick curd, whisked

1 tsp garam masala powder

2 tsp red chilli powder

2 tsp salt

½ tsp turmeric powder

1 tbsp chopped coriander leaves

- Wash chicken, pat dry and cut into 3" cubes.

- Combine ingredients for marinade to a smooth paste, rub into chicken and marinate for 30 minutes.

- Heat oil in a non-stick pan, add garlic and ginger and fry lightly.

- Add onions and fry till brown.

- Reduce heat, add poppy seeds, cheronji, cashew nuts and coconut, and fry for a few seconds.

- Stir in tomato purée and cook till masala is well fried and oil starts to bubble on top.

- Add chicken with its marinade and lime juice.

- Cover pan and cook over low heat for 25 minutes, stirring occasionally till chicken is tender and gravy is thick.

Rice

- Wash rice and soak in water for 30 minutes.

- Cook rice in plenty of water with salt till three-quarters done. Drain and allow rice to cool.

1 tbsp chopped green chillies

1 tbsp chopped mint leaves

Rice
1/2 kg (2 1/2 cups) basmati rice

1 tsp salt

1/4 tsp saffron soaked in 1/3 cup warm milk

1/4 tsp yellow or red food colouring (optional)

1 tbsp ghee

- Place one-third of the rice in a deep pan or ovenproof dish. Place half the chicken over the rice. Cover with another one-third rice. Place remaining chicken over rice and cover with remaining rice.

- Mix food colouring (if used), with saffron-flavoured milk and sprinkle with ghee on top.

- Cook on dum or bake in an oven preheated to 180°C (350°C) for 30-40 minutes.

- Serve with curd and kachumber.

Note: Please be sure to use food colour from a recognized and reputed brand.

Variation: Sultanas (kishmish), peeled and slivered almonds and grated coconut can be sprinkled on the rice before baking.

KEEMA NAAN
Naan stuffed with Chicken Mince

Makes: 6

Dough
½ kg flour (maida)

¼ tsp baking powder

½ tsp salt

1 cup warm milk

1 cup curd, whisked

¾ egg, lightly beaten

1 tsp ghee

Filling
2 tbsp oil

½ tsp garlic paste

½ tsp ginger paste

200 gms chicken mince

¾ tsp red chilli powder

½ tsp garam masala powder

¼ tsp turmeric powder

¾ tsp salt

¾ cup fresh tomato purée

1 medium onion, chopped

1 tbsp chopped coriander leaves

1 tbsp chopped green chillies

- Mix all ingredients for dough and knead to a soft dough.

- Cover and leave aside for 3-4 hours.

- Heat oil for filling in a non-stick pan and lightly fry garlic and ginger.

- Add chicken and fry till pale gold, stirring continuously.

- Stir in powdered spices and salt, and fry for a few seconds.

- Add tomato purée and continue frying till oil starts to bubble on top.

- Remove from heat, stir in onion, coriander leaves and green chillies, and allow to cool.

- Divide dough into 6 portions.

- Flatten each portion into a disc 3" in diameter. Place a portion of filling in the centre of the disc. Fold over dough to cover filling and pinch to seal. Shape into a flat round and roll out on a floured surface into a 6" round naan.

- Lightly beat egg and milk for topping and brush top of each naan with mixture. Sprinkle with poppy and nigella seeds.

Topping

¼ egg

1 tbsp milk

1 tbsp nigella seeds (kalaunji)

1 tbsp poppy seeds (khus-khus)

- Grill in an electric grill preheated to 220°C (425°F) for 3-4 minutes. Turn over and grill for 2 minutes more. (If your grill is not graded in degrees, then grill at maximum temperature for 3-4 minutes.)

- Naan can also be baked in an oven preheated to 220°C (425°F) for 3 minutes.

Variations:

Eggless Keema Naan: *Omit the egg and use ⅓ cup extra curd to knead the dough. Add extra water if needed.*

Keema Paratha: *Make a dough with 5 cups whole wheat flour (atta) and 3½ cups water. Cover with a damp cloth and leave to rest for an hour. Prepare the filling and make 6 paratha, each 6" in diameter. Roast paratha on a heated tava, till light brown on both sides. Smear with butter or ghee on both sides to make it crisp.*

Fat-free Paratha: *Grill parathé in an electric grill preheated to 220°C (425°F) for 3-4 minutes on each side.*

accompaniments

SIRKÉ KA PYAZ
Pickled Onions

¼ kg small Madras or
pickling onions

2 cups white vinegar

1 tsp salt

1 tsp sugar

1 slice beetroot

- Peel onions. Wash and dry.

- Mix remaining ingredients, add onions and keep covered for 12 hours.

- Remove onions and serve with any chicken preparation.

LACHHEDAR PYAZ
Sliced Onion Relish

Makes: 2 cups

2 medium onions

½ small beetroot or
carrot

1 tbsp finely chopped
mint

1 tbsp finely chopped
coriander leaves

¼ tsp salt

Juice of 1 large lime

- Slice onions and beetroot or carrot very fine.

- Soak onion slices in iced water for 20 minutes. Remove and drain.

- Toss in remaining ingredients.

- Serve with barbecued chicken, kababs or biryani.

HARA DHANIA AUR NARIAL KI CHUTNEY

Coriander and Coconut Chutney

Makes: About 2 cups

3 cups chopped coriander leaves

1 medium, fresh coconut, grated

1 tbsp roasted cumin seeds

1 tbsp roasted groundnuts

6 green chillies, chopped

2 tbsp sugar

1/2 tbsp salt

Juice of 2 limes

- Wash coriander leaves and green chillies, and pat dry.

- Mix all ingredients and grind to a paste.

- This chutney can be frozen for months.

PUDINA CHUTNEY

Mint Chutney

Makes: About 1 cup

1 cup mint leaves

1/2 cup chopped coriander leaves

1 medium onion

1/2 tsp garlic paste

2 green chillies, chopped

1/2 tsp sugar or 1 tsp jaggery

1/2 tsp salt

1 tsp fresh lime juice

1 tsp dry pomegranate seeds (anardana)

- Wash mint and coriander leaves, and pat dry.

- Grind all ingredients to a smooth paste.

- Store in an airtight jar and preserve in the refrigerator. It will stay for a week.

Note: This chutney mixed with a little curd makes a delicious accompaniment for tandoori tikka and kabab.

MURGH KA ACHAAR
Chicken Pickle

1 kg boneless chicken

200 gms (scant 1 cup) mustard oil

1/2 tsp asafoetida powder (hing)

6-8 pungent dried red chillies

1 1/2 tsp fenugreek seeds (methi)

6-7 black cardamoms

6-7 x 1" sticks cinnamon

6-7 black peppercorns

1 1/2 tsp red chilli powder

1 1/2 tsp salt

400 gms (3 large) onions, sliced

50 gms garlic (3 bulbs), sliced

50 gms ginger (4" piece), sliced

25 gms (10 tsp) roasted aniseed (saunf)

1 1/2 tsp garam masala powder

1 cup brown vinegar

- Wash chicken, pat dry and cut into 3" cubes.

- Heat oil in a pan to smoking point.

- Reduce heat and add asafoetida. Stir and add red chillies and fenugreek seeds. Fry for a few seconds.

- Add whole spices, chilli powder, salt and chicken. Fry for 5 minutes stirring constantly.

- Add onions and garlic. Cover pan and cook till oil starts to bubble on top.

- Stir in ginger, aniseed, garam masala and vinegar.

- Bring to boil and remove from heat immediately.

- Cool and bottle.

Note: Preferably, keep the pickle in the refrigerator. It will stay for 2-3 months.

LACHHEDAR PUDINA PARATHA
Mint Paratha

Makes: 12-14

Dough
1/2 kg flour (maida)

1 tbsp ghee

1/2 tsp salt

1 cup chopped mint leaves

Lining
2 tbsp ghee

2 tbsp flour (maida)

- Combine all ingredients for dough with enough water and knead into a soft dough.

- Cover with a damp cloth and leave for an hour.

- Heat 2 tbsp ghee for lining in a pan and fry flour over low heat till it becomes a pale gold paste. Cool.

- Divide dough into 12-14 portions, roll each portion into a thin roti and spread some of the lining over each.

- Roll roti into a sausage and roll sausage into a pinwheel, keeping the folded edges on the outer side.

- Place pinwheel flat on a floured board and roll into a thick roti.

- Roast in a regular clay or gas tandoor, or bake in an oven preheated to 220°C (425°F) for 5 minutes.

TANDOORI ROTI

Makes: 10

¼ kg whole wheat flour (atta)

¼ tsp salt

- Mix flour and salt with a little water and knead into soft dough. Cover with a damp cloth and leave for an hour.

- Divide dough into 10 portions and roll out each portion into a thick roti.

- Bake in a regular clay or gas tandoor, or in an electric oven preheated to 220°C (425°F) for 5 minutes.

Note: Try to use minimum flour while rolling the roti.

ROOMALI ROTI

Makes: 20-24 medium roti

The word roomali means handkerchief. The roti is soft and pliable, just like a handkerchief and is as light as a feather. Roomali roti is an excellent accompaniment with all varieties of barbecued boneless meat and kabab.

1 kg flour (maida)

150 gms (3/4 cup) semolina

½ cup oil

1½ cups milk

1 tsp salt

1½ cups water

- Combine all ingredients except water. Adding a little water at a time and knead into a soft dough.

- Cover with a damp cloth and leave for an hour.

- Divide dough into small portions and roll each into a paper-thin roti.

- Place an inverted tava or gridle on heat. When tava is hot, place a roti on it.

- Roast for 2 minutes. As soon as bubbles appear on the surface, turn roti and cook for a minute longer. The roti should be soft.

- Fold into four and serve immediately.

Note: Roomali roti can also be covered with foil to keep it warm, as it becomes dry and leathery when cold.

PLAIN PULAO

Serves: 2

1 cup basmati rice
3 tbsp oil
1" stick cinnamon
2 black cardamoms
2 cloves
1 bay leaf (tej patta)
1 tsp salt
1/4 tsp turmeric powder
2 cups chicken stock or water

- Wash rice and soak in water for 20 minutes. Drain.

- Heat oil in a non-stick pan, add whole spices and bay leaf, and fry lightly till fragrant.

- Reduce heat, add rice, turmeric and salt, and fry for 8-9 minutes.

- Transfer rice into a deep pan, add chicken stock or water, cover pan and simmer on minimum heat till rice is tender and dry.

- Discard whole spices and bay leaf, if desired, before serving.

glossary

ENGLISH	HINDI	ENGLISH	HINDI
Almond	Badam	Kidney beans	Rajma
Aniseed	Chhoti saunf	Lime	Neebu
Apricot	Khurbani	Liver	Kaleji
Asafoetida	Hing	Mace	Javitri
Baking soda	Meetha soda	Mango	Aam
Bay leaf	Tej patta	Mango - raw, dried	Aamchur
Bengal gram - flour	Besan	Milk	Doodh
Bengal gram - green	Hara chana	Milk condensed -	
Bengal gram - husked	Chana dal	unsweetened	Khoya
Bengal gram - roasted	Bhuné chané	Mince	Keema
Black beans - husked	Urud dal	Mint	Pudina
Black pepper	Kali mirch	Mustard	Rai / sarson
Black salt	Kala namak	Nigella seeds	Kalaunji
Butter	Makhan	Nutmeg	Jaiphal
Butter - clarified	Ghee	Onion	Pyaz
Capsicum	Shimla mirch	Orange	Santra
Caraway seeds	Shah jeera	Papaya - raw	Kaccha papeeta
Cardamom - black	Badi elaichi	Pigeon peas	Arhar / Toover
Cardamom - green	Chhoti elaichi	Pine nuts	Chilgoza
Carrot	Gaajar	Pineapple	Annanas
Cashew nut	Kaju	Pistachio nuts	Pista
Cauliflower	Phool gobi	Pomegranate seeds	Anardana
Chicken	Murgh	Poppy seeds	Khus-khus
Chilli	Mirch	Potato	Alu
Cinnamon	Dalchini	Radish	Mooli
Clove	Laung	Rice	Chawal
Coconut - dried	Copra	Rose-water	Gulabjal
Coconut - fresh	Nariyal	Saffron	Kesar / Zafran
Coriander	Dhania	Salt	Namak
Corn	Makkai	Screwpine flower	
Cottage cheese	Paneer	essence	Kewra
Cucumber	Kheera	Semolina	Sooji / Rava
Cumin seeds	Jeera	Sesame	Til
Curd	Dahi	Silver leaf	Chandi ka varak
Curry leaf	Kari patta	Spinach	Palak
Date	Khajoor	Star anise	Badian
Dill	Sua	Sugar	Cheeni
Egg	Anda	Sultana	Kishmish
Fennel	Badi saunf	Tamarind	Imli
Fenugreek	Methi	Tomato	Tamatar
Fenugreek leaves - dried	Kasuri methi	Turmeric	Haldi
Fig	Anjeer	Vinegar	Sirka
Flour - refined	Maida	Walnut	Akhrot
Flour - whole wheat	Atta	Wheat	Gehun
Garlic	Lehsun	Yoghurt	Substitute for curd
Ginger - dried	Saunth		
Ginger - fresh	Adrak		
Green peas	Matar		
Honey	Madh / Shahad		
Jaggery	Gur		
Kidney	Gurda		

Char Magaz: A mixture of water melon, marsh melon, cucumber and pumpkin seeds.

Kokum: A dry sour plum – the botanical name is *Garcina indica*.